STEPS TO
CHRISTIAN UNDERSTANDING

STEPS TO
CHRISTIAN
UNDERSTANDING

Edited by

R. J. W. BEVAN

NEW YORK
OXFORD UNIVERSITY PRESS
LONDON   TORONTO
1958

Oxford University Press, Amen House, London E.C.4

GLASGOW   NEW YORK   TORONTO   MELBOURNE   WELLINGTON
BOMBAY   CALCUTTA   MADRAS   KARACHI   KUALA LUMPUR
CAPE TOWN   IBADAN   NAIROBI   ACCRA

Printed in Great Britain by
Spottiswoode, Ballantyne and Co. Ltd.
London and Colchester

FOREWORD

THE Editor of this book, like many other men and women in his profession, is concerned with the teaching of religion and philosophy in a Secondary School; but unlike the majority of Secondary School teachers, he is on the staff of a Technical High School and is (he believes) one of the few who teach Scripture in a Technical School in Britain. It is a commonplace that we live in an age when technical and scientific education is supremely important to a nation, and when more and more of the future citizens of all countries are going to be technically minded; at the same time it is widely said that man's ability and powers in applied science and engineering have far outstripped his moral and religious insight. Moreover, as has been remarked (in a second leader in *The Times*, 12 October, 1957), there is a keen appetite for religious discussion, though that often takes place on a very inadequate basis of knowledge.

Discussion of such matters as the existence of a personal God, creation, the Incarnation of God in a human being, the existence and personality of the Holy Spirit, involves difficult questions for the layman whose training is concerned with quite different kinds of subject. Young people, or those of any age who are young in mind, who are ready to discuss such topics frankly and sincerely, should not be warned off as if these questions were too deep for them, but they need guidance and help if they are to see the issues involved and adopt intelligent attitudes. Too often, it has been said, people think they have rejected Christian claims when in fact they have never known sufficient about Christianity to reject it with understanding.

The distinguished contributors who have given of their time and energy to supply the chapters which follow, have here offered such guidance in written form. All are Christians, and it is hoped that their work, arranged as it is on a definite plan, may provide for some readers positive 'Steps to Christian Understanding'. At any rate it should help to spread clearer information about the Christian position, as it is held by this group of educated people, including both Anglicans and members of non-episcopal churches, laymen as well as clergy, and scientists as well as humanists and theologians.

The Plan of the Book

It will be seen that there are three sections, I, 'God and the World', II, 'God and Man', III, 'Doctrines of the Christian Faith'. There is a logical sequence in this order. In the Christian view the world is God's world, and therefore has a real meaning. But this meaning must be looked for, not in the world, which is material, but in man, who is moral and spiritual. Through Christ and his death and resurrection, man has been brought into a new relationship with God, and therefore the Incarnation marks a turning point in the history of mankind.

The Christian Religion is concerned with ultimate facts about reality and existence. They assume significance only when seen in the context of the eternal and spiritual rather than the merely temporal and finite order. But since we live within the setting of the physical world, and since we are most immediately aware of ourselves, it is the world and man in their relation to God which form our first objects of interest and study. Christianity, like other religions, has its own particular beliefs about the meaning of the universe and the place of man in creation. Therefore the first two sections, I, 'God and the World', and II, 'God and Man', are closely related. This is entirely in line with the biblical view, for when we consider the earliest and also the most persistent idea in the Old Testament, it is that of the 'triangular' relationship between God, man and the universe. The biblical account of creation is firmly based on the belief in a *personal* creator. The world did not happen by chance, but owes its origin and continuance to the power and working of God. Man is the highest of all creatures and our material surroundings are the result of God's creative activity. The universe is not a mere 'fortuitous concurrence of atoms', but an ordered and comprehensible unity, possessing that mode of being and reality, which seemed good to God, when he brought the universe into existence.

It is on this basis that we proceed to Section III, 'Doctrines of the Christian Faith', which deals with crucial Christian doctrines.

The supreme biblical theme is the revelation of God. God must be self-declared, for man has no scientific instruments or devices which can search out God. The important question is, 'How is God to reveal himself?' The first two sections have already shown that God reveals himself, though not exhaustively, through nature and history. 'The heavens declare the glory of God, and the firmament sheweth his handywork.' God also inspired chosen men who were his instruments for the revelation of the divine purpose. These were the prophets who, though full of a sense of their personal weakness, yet declared the 'Word of the Lord', in spite of their initial hesitancy and misgiving.

Finally, as we see in the third section, 'God, who at sundry times and in divers manners spake in time past unto the fathers by the prophets, hath in these last days spoken unto us by his Son'. Jesus Christ is the supreme and unique revelation of God. 'The only begotten Son which is in the bosom of the Father, He hath declared Him'. There are other religions also with a verifiable historical basis, but nowhere else can anything be found comparable with the pattern of events leading up to and converging upon the Incarnation.

The importance of the historical facts of the earthly life of Jesus is derived from their theological or doctrinal meaning. It is the Christian belief that he is the eternal Son of God, and that we see 'the light of the knowledge of the glory of God in the face of Jesus Christ'. 'The Word was made flesh and dwelt among us', the full and final manifestation of God to men. The Incarnation is the centre of God's activity in history, and, the doctrine of the Incarnation is the central doctrine of Christianity.

It is inseparably connected with the doctrines of the Holy Spirit and the Trinity. In the experience of the Christian Church belief in the deity of the Father and of the Son was accompanied by belief in the deity of the Holy Spirit, and this led to belief in the three distinct persons of the Godhead. How did this come about? Beginning with the Jewish belief in the One Creator God, 'there was also the fact of Jesus, who was a person such as they could treat only as God' (see page 169).

An examination of the life and experience of the early Christian Church as described in the New Testament discloses a further point. 'The Holy Spirit was not regarded as a force or an influence, but always as a person. He is represented as a person, distinct from the Father and the Son, and a study of the activities attributed to him, and the authority which he is recognized as possessing shows that he is regarded as a divine person' (page 170).

So the doctrine of the Trinity emerged as a result of personal experience, when 'it was seen that the only way to do justice to the whole of Christian truth was to recognize that God is both three and One' (page 172).

If the Creation is a natural starting point of Christian thought, a fitting conclusion is the consideration of what happens at the end of the world and of time. The early Christians lived in vivid expectation of the second coming of Christ and confidently hoped for the resurrection of the dead. The centre of the Christian hope in the New Testament was fixed on 'the day of the Lord'. His second coming on the final Lord's Day meant his real presence, and the more they realized his presence on earth, the more they looked forward to his presence on that day.

Our hope is the Christian hope, and it is focused on an event and a meeting. It is a corporate hope, which belongs to all Christians, not a mere selfish search for private and individual salvation. On this side, there is growth, preparation, and expectation, but there will come journey's end, fulfilment, and consummation. Death is the boundary which limits the range of human development in this life, but beyond it there are endless possibilities which we cannot at present imagine.

The above is the principal theme of Parts I–III, and at the end of the book Dr. Nathaniel Micklem sums up, in a valuable conclusion, the most important lines of thought suggested by the contributors.

I should like to mention here my indebtedness to the authorities of the Oxford University Press, from whom I have received unfailing patience, courtesy and consideration, which I have found most helpful and encouraging. I have been specially helped by several valuable suggestions regarding the plan and scope of the book.

Finally, I acknowledge my deep gratitude to the contributors, whose generous co-operation has made my task such a happy one. They readily consented to the appearance of their respective essays within these covers, because of their real desire to assist in the promoting of Christian understanding.

R.J.W.B.

Burnley Technical High School
December 1957

CONTENTS

PART III: DOCTRINES OF THE CHRISTIAN FAITH

CONCLUSION

INTRODUCTION

Thinking about Religion

W. R. MATTHEWS

MANY persons do not think about religion, some because it does not seem to them worth thinking about and others because they are satisfied to accept without question the beliefs and practices in which they have been brought up. There are even those who hold that it is wrong to think about it; they say, 'We leave that to the experts', by which they often mean that they follow the teaching of the Church without much effort to understand what it means. Most intelligent persons, however, at some time in their lives have felt the need for some thought about religion, for no one can deny that religion exists and has played a remarkable part in the history of mankind, nor can they deny that, if there is any truth in religion, it must concern them and could quite possibly be a dominating force in their lives.

Thinking is always a process of asking questions and trying to find the most satisfying answers, but thinking can become confused and futile if we do not take care to ask the really important questions and, so far as possible, get them in the right order. In this essay, I aim at suggesting what are the fundamental questions. I shall refer to some of the answers which have been given, but my chief purpose is to lay out the ground which I think has to be covered. It is a very wide field and anyone who set out to explore the whole of it thoroughly would find that a life-time was all too short to complete his task. This ought not to discourage us, but we may at least beware of supposing that we shall be able to clear up all the problems. It is not likely that we shall be fortunate enough to answer all our questions with complete certainty. The man who hopes that by thinking hard enough he will be in a position to dispense with faith is deluding himself. What we may hope is that our faith will become a reasonable faith—not blind but enlightened.

The first question which presents itself is: What is Religion? It seems obvious that before we begin to think about religion we ought to have some clear idea of what we are thinking about. When we study triangles, we have at least a general notion of what a triangle is, and when we study Biology we start with a vague conception of what is meant by living beings. It has turned out that the question What is Religion? is extraordinarily difficult. There are at least a hundred well-known definitions of religion, none of which has gained general acceptance. The reason for this is, of course, that the word 'religion' is used to cover such a wide diversity of beliefs and practices, from the worship of 'fetishes' and of animals and spirits, to the highest spiritual worship by great saints and philosophers. It has proved impossible to invent a formula which would include this measureless diversity. Nor can we say 'Well, even if we cannot define Religion, we recognize it when we see it.' For at one end of the scale of values Religion and Magic are not easily distinguished from one another and at the other end we are sometimes puzzled to draw the line between Religion and Philosophy.

Aristotle insisted that the nature of anything could be discovered only by finding out what it could become—its potentiality. This principle is important when we are studying Religion, because it prevents us from falling into what might be called the 'Nothing but' fallacy. It may be true, though it is by no means certain, that religion first appeared on the earth in an extremely crude and superstitious form, and it may be true that we can trace a development, or even an 'evolution', of religion from that lowly beginning, but it would be foolish to argue that a highly developed form of religion, such as Christianity, is in any important respect identical with that embryo stage. One hears, for example, at times the allegation that there is a resemblance between the Christian Eucharist and the sacrificial meal of tribes who eat their totem animal and that, therefore, the Christian sacrament is 'nothing but' a refined totemism. The truth is, of course, that the resemblances, though real, are superficial, while the difference in meaning and context is profound.

I think we ought to be careful in using the conception of 'evolution'. It is a word which needs definition and, unless we know precisely what we mean by it, may prevent us from asking some most necessary questions. The word 'evolution' may mean simply that there has been a development; it becomes explanatory only when we have some theory of the cause of this development. In Biology there are indeed alleged causes of evolution; in the study of Religion we have no such principle as natural selection to guide our research—or at least it would not take us very far in that field.

We may conclude from all this that we must seek for an understanding of religion first of all by looking at it in its highest and most mature manifestations. We shall not learn very much about it by concentrating on Fetish Worship or Animism any more than we should learn much about the nature of Natural Science by an intensive study of Alchemy. And, when we turn to the great religions of the world, we seem to find that, with all their profound differences, there is an even more profound kinship, and that this kinship becomes more obvious when we study the noblest expressions of each religion. The saints and wise men of all the great religions are surprisingly alike in spirit and in conduct, though their creeds may be far apart.

Perhaps, then, it may be most fruitful to ask whether there is such a thing as religious experience which can be recognized and even, to some extent, defined? In all the many religions and religious persons can we distinguish some common element or some common attitude? No doubt psychology can help us to answer this question, but I doubt whether it can take us all the way. We shall come to a question, in the end, on which psychology has nothing to say—the nature of man and of the Universe of which he is both a part and a spectator. However this may be, the problem of the nature of religious experience is worth considering and some interesting suggestions are before us. I will mention two only. The first is that religion is a 'feeling of absolute dependence'. This idea, which was propounded by Schleiermacher, is historically important, because it has exercised considerable influence on other thinkers and it is at least partly right. Dependence certainly enters deeply into religious experience of every kind. The first step in religion, one might almost say, is the apprehension that we are not either the 'masters of our fate' or the 'captains of our soul'. We have no space to discuss Schleiermacher's view here. Anyone who thinks it out will probably feel that he wants to amend it by adding something, perhaps the element of belief. Rudolf Otto's book, *The Idea of the Holy*, should be read by everyone who takes the study of religion seriously, not only because it contains a reasoned statement of a theory of the essential nature of religious experience, but also because it is the work of a writer who had an intimate knowledge of Eastern religion as well as of Christian theology. Otto has introduced a word into the discussion which often occurs in books written since his *Idea of the Holy* appeared—the 'Numinous'. He holds that 'the sense of the Numinous' is the core of religion in all its forms from the lowest to the highest. The sense of the Numinous is indefinable. It has some affinity with fear, but it differs from ordinary fear in that it includes the element of 'fascination'; in it are mingled, so to say, dread and longing. This numinous sense animates the worshipper of stocks and stones, but it becomes awe and reverence in the spiritual devotion of a St. Augustine.

The reader, no doubt, has already been conscious of an apparent gap in these theories of religion. Where, he may ask, is the belief which seems to be necessary for any kind of religion? Neither Schleiermacher nor Otto, of course, were foolish enough to ignore this factor, and each deals with it in his own way, but it must be owned that they are least satisfactory in their treatment of the intellectual aspect of religion—its believing side. And this is evidently important. Every religion appears to assert, or imply, some propositions about the world and about human life, and it is for this reason that we are able to use the words 'true' and 'false' about religions. We could hardly do so if religion were nothing else than a way of feeling. Our Christian religion has a body of doctrine, that is of statements which are presented to our minds as true, and at the head of them stands the majestic, 'I believe in God', on which all the rest depend. It is natural for Christians to suppose that all other religions must have some similar doctrine of God, but this is not the case. In many of the lower religions one could find no explicit belief about Deity, and in the more primitive form of Buddhism, the 'Hinayana', there is no doctrine of God.

While recognizing, however, that the history of religion forbids us to say quite simply that religion means belief in God, we may justly remark that religious aspiration and worship seem to be directed upon some Object and are often felt as being the human response to that Object. The development of the idea of Deity is a long and complicated story which we cannot trace here, but it is relevant to point out that it raises a fundamental question for our consideration. How are we to interpret this development? The question comes to us most forcibly when we think of that part of the history of religion which is best known to us through the Bible. The Hebrews certainly passed through a process of religious development in which the tribal God became transformed into the righteous and holy God of the whole earth. There are two possible interpretations of these facts. We may regard them as wholly explicable by the circumstances of the history of the Hebrews and by the growth of the ethical consciousness and the critical intelligence, or we may, while admitting that these causes affected the course of development, attribute the whole movement to the action of God and see in it a progressive revelation. Obviously, this question goes to the root of the problem and the answer which we give to it will guide our attitude to all religious phenomena. I will make one observation on this. The men who were the chief instruments in the development of the idea of God, the Prophets, were quite certain that the word which they spoke was the word which came to them from God; it was revelation. I do not say that this is decisive, for they might have been mistaken, but I do assert that their belief deserves respectful consideration, for, after all, if they had not believed it there would have been no progress in religion to study. *Prima facie* the man who has an experience may be expected to know what it is better than one who has never had anything of the kind. If we accept the idea of progressive revelation, we can hardly escape the further question of the extent of this principle. Are we to suppose that there is only one authentic Revelation, that recorded in the Christian Scriptures, or shall we expect to find revelation in other religions recorded in other scriptures?

Here we touch upon a problem that has divided Christian thinkers in the past and still, in a more sophisticated form, is the subject of controversy. It must be owned that, on the whole, the weight of Christian opinion has been in favour of the narrower view. The prevailing doctrine has been that all religions, except the Christian and its Hebrew forerunner, are false and that their deities are pure illusions or, more probably, devils. Some of the early Christian Fathers, however, did not exclude the possibility that there had been a revelation to some of the heathen and even held that some of

the great Greek thinkers prepared the way for Christ.
Such writers as Clement of Alexandria and Origen were
deeply indebted to Plato and could not doubt that he
had received some glimpse of divine truth. Augustine,
too, was brought to faith in Christ through Platonism.
We must observe, however, that it was Greek philosophy
and not Greek religion which seemed to them worthy of
respect. Augustine's contemptuous criticism of pagan
religion in the *City of God* represents the common attitude of educated Christians in the early centuries and
throughout the Middle Ages. It is worthy of note that
the exclusive standpoint with regard to other religions
is characteristic of the two world religions which have
inherited their belief in God from Judaism with its
'jealous' God—Christianity and the Moslem faith—
while Hinduism and Buddhism have been more tolerant.
It must unfortunately be admitted that religious persecution has been more frequent in those regions which
have acknowledged Christ or Mohammed than in the
Far East.

The conclusion to which we adhere on the extent of
divine revelation has a direct bearing on another question which is much debated. Shall we approach the study
of Christianity on the assumption that, provisionally at
least, it is just one of the great religions of the world, or
shall we start with the assumption that it is, *sui generis*,
the absolute religion? This may seem an academic problem of no great practical interest, but in fact it is the
point where two ways of thinking about religion divide.
The 'History of Religions' school would regard Christianity as possibly the highest development of religion,
but at the same time as a stage in a process of evolution,
to be 'explained' in part by its place in the process. Many

theologians today would count this method as inadmissible and as a betrayal of the Christian faith. Karl Barth, for example, would hold that the sole business of Christian theologians is to expound and set out in order the implications of the Revelation in Christ. It appears to me that there is truth in both these points of view. Certainly it is the primary duty of every Christian thinker to understand his own religion, and we shall do little good if we make a superficial survey of other religions before we have made an earnest attempt to grapple intellectually with our own. But, at the same time, Christianity quite obviously *is* a religion and there *are* others; it cannot surely be foolish to compare them and to study the relations between them. It may be that we shall gain from such a study not only enlightenment, but a confirmation of our faith, for it would be a strong support for the claim of the Christian religion if it could be shown that the spiritual quests of all religions find in it their fulfilment.

We have seen that the problems presented to our minds by the study of religion are not confined to that of the existence and nature of God, but it must also be evident that this problem forces itself upon our attention. In principle, we have already raised it when we touched upon religious experience, for the truly vital question with regard to religious experience is whether or not it is a kind of persistent illusion. As everyone knows, Freud and many of his disciples claim to have shown on psychological grounds that this is precisely what it is. To refute this opinion, we do not have to argue that illusion has not played a part in the history of religion—that indeed would be a desperate enterprise—but we have to defend the proposition that religious experience is experience of something, or of Someone, and that there is a Reality which calls out the experience; in short that religion is a response and not a purely subjective aberration of the human mind. We have to maintain that, with all the mistakes and absurdities which religious beliefs and practices have manifested when religious men have tried to express in images, ideas and actions what they felt or believed about the divine, they were reacting to something, some Being which is truly there. And this means that we must ask the question, Is it reasonable to believe in God?

A remarkable fact about this question is that it is never explicitly raised in the Bible. There is no such thing in our Scriptures as an argument to prove the reality of God and this is true of most of the other sacred writings of the world. The Hebrews did not reason logically on the problem of deity. The Bible comes before us not as religious philosophy but as revelation and, whatever else that may mean, it means at least that it is the record of religious experience. It was the Greeks, with their genius for reasoning, who began the long argument on the being and nature of God. In the Christian religion, the two streams, that from Palestine and that from Hellas, have flowed together and reflection has begun from, or been guided by, the Hebrew experience and its culmination in Jesus, which has been accepted as revelation. At first sight, it may seem that this blending of reason and revelation is a faulty method of approach and that the problem should be dealt with on purely rational grounds as one of metaphysics. Further consideration, however, will persuade us, I think, that this is not the case. The question, Does God exist? arises out of religious experience. But for the fact that religion has been, and is, a powerful factor in human life and that men do have feelings of awe and reverence and know the need for worship there would be nothing to suggest the question, or, if that is too extreme a statement, it would not have the urgency which it certainly possesses. The question at issue is really whether or not the whole of religious experience is what Mr. Ford said of history—'bunk'.

One important suggestion seems to follow with regard to the so-called 'proofs' or arguments for the existence of God. We should never separate them from the background of religious experience. Regarded as isolated trains of reasoning, they may seem to fail in reaching irrefragable conclusions; they may appear in a more favourable light if we regard them as efforts of the mind to understand and explain something which seems to be given in man's apprehension of himself and his total environment.

At the present time, philosophical arguments on the existence of God have to meet an objection at the outset. Logical Positivists would tell us that the sentences 'God exists' and 'God does not exist' are non-sense—they have no meaning, and, therefore, our question is not really a question at all. The ground on which they base this astonishing assertion is the view which they adopt of meaning. Nothing has meaning, they hold, in the logical sense except statements which could be verified, or disproved, by some sense-experience, and since the assertion 'God is' obviously cannot be verified in this way, it is unmeaning. We may, I think, dismiss this objection on several grounds. The theory is derived from one specialized kind of investigation—the experimental method of science—and is difficult to apply to other kinds of research, e.g. historical. It is most improbable, surely, that all the thought which has been directed on this question should have been occupied with a problem which is simply a mistake—a pseudo-problem. But we need not heap up refutations, for the Logical Positivist theory on 'the meaning of meaning' refutes itself. It resembles the theory of absolute scepticism in this respect: The man who says, 'I know that I can know nothing', contradicts himself in one breath; in much the same way anyone who says, 'All statements which cannot be verified by some sense-experience are non-sense,' may be invited to point to any such experience which could verify that statement. Obviously he cannot, and thus, on his own principle, the statement is meaningless.

The mass of writing on the subject of the Being of God is so vast that it is easy to lose one's way in all the discussions, histories of the arguments, and related issues. Probably the best plan for any student would be to read the classical presentations of the great arguments and to master them in their primitive simplicity before going on to the complications of criticism and controversy. The material for this has been collected in a useful volume, *Selections from the Literature of Theism*, by Caldecott and Mackintosh, with the notes and explanations needed by a novice to guide his attention to the salient points.

The three classical arguments should be the centre of our inquiry into the question of the rationality of belief in God and, even if we finally reject them all, we ought to have some clear reasons for rejecting reasoning which has satisfied so many acute minds. Let us beware of the fallacy of fashion in thinking. One may hear today that the Theistic Arguments are 'outmoded'. What a curious reproach on the lips of a philosopher who professes to be guided by reason and not by the opinions of the contemporary majority! We shall be well advised to do our own thinking on this matter.

We cannot here even touch upon the substance of the Theistic Arguments, but a few comments may not be entirely useless. The Ontological Argument, which argues from the Idea of God in the mind to the reality of God, should be studied first in its original formulation by St. Anselm before we go on to notice its modifications by later thinkers. I have noticed that persons tend to react to this argument when it first comes before them in two opposite ways: they either dismiss it as a mere playing on words or they accept it as plainly and finally conclusive. Neither reaction is well-founded. The number of philosophers of the first rank who have adopted the Ontological Argument in some form refutes the first, and the number of equally acute thinkers who have considered and discarded it refutes the second.

Most philosophical defences of Theism are based upon the Cosmological Argument in one of its many forms. As its name implies, it is essentially a chain of reasoning from the existence of the world to God and it has often been stated as the argument to the First Cause. This is by no means the only way of presenting it and probably not the best. The essence of the Cosmological Argument is the demonstration that the world of finite things and events is not a self-explanatory system and that, if we press our inquiry, insisting on asking the last question, we are led to the necessary conception of Eternal Mind on which all things depend. It is important to grasp the real meaning of this argument because many today are under the impression that if science goes on with its researches it will eventually answer all our questions. No doubt it will answer a great many questions—and raise many more—but it can never answer the question why there is anything at all, why there is a universe.

The Teleological Argument, often called the Argument from Design, is really a corollary of the Cosmological Argument. It reasons from the signs of purpose in the world to the Mind of a Creator. We still come across men who suppose that the theory of evolution has finally refuted this kind of proof, and we must own that the rather simple-minded reasonings from the structure of the eye and similar examples of apparent purpose which used to be popular with apologists for religion have lost their force. It is, however, very far from being true that the Teleological Argument has been destroyed by Evolution. Before we accept that conclusion we must ask what precisely is meant by the word 'Evolution'. We shall find that it is a most ambiguous term and only in one sense, which few scientists would adopt today, does it rule out the idea of purposiveness. We may see reason to think that the evolution of mind, to take the most fundamental aspect of the problem, suggests very strongly the purposive direction of Creative Mind.[1]

For many modern minds the 'moral argument' carries greater weight than the three which we have treated as the 'classical' proofs. In this they agree with Kant, who, after exposing what he held to be their fallacy, turned to moral experience as the sufficient basis for belief in God, Freedom and Immortality. To the plain man it may well seem that he is on firmer ground when he starts from the common conviction that there is a clear distinction between right and wrong, that duty has an absolute claim upon us and that we have the responsibility and the

[1] I have discussed this in my book, *The Purpose of God* (Nisbet).

power to choose good rather than evil. When we try to express, however, this intuition in the form of a coherent argument we discover that the task is not easy. This is due to the fact that, though moral experience undoubtedly forms an integral part of the life of every sane human being, there are several different ways of interpreting it. There are many types of ethical theory, and much will depend on which we adopt. Some of these theories appear rather to 'explain away' our moral experience than to draw out its implications, and obviously such theories will not lend themselves to form the starting point of an argument for the being of God. You may account for the sense of moral obligation in two ways: you may try to show that the sense of obligation is a mistake due to psychological causes which reach back into the social evolution of mankind, useful no doubt, but not significant of the nature of reality, or you may try to show that the sense of moral obligation is only to be accounted for by the belief that there is an Eternal Good, or a God of righteousness. The moral argument in all its forms presupposes that we take moral experience seriously and as having authority which we cannot disregard. Unfortunately, today, many of our contemporaries are not prepared to make this assumption and perhaps the only answer to them is to point out that their scepticism with regard to moral obligation undermines the dignity and value of the human person.

Moral values are not the only values, and any full philosophy of Theism would have much to say about Truth and Beauty. We must not pursue this intricate question here, but we may remark that all thought about religion is bound to keep steadily in mind that the universe is not only the system of events which science progressively exposes to our understanding, it is also a sphere in which values are sought, realized and expressed. Love, the devotion to truth, beauty and goodness are as real as—are in fact probably far more real than—electrons. The God in whom we can believe is not only the Creator of the physical universe; he is the Supreme Value—the Eternal Good and the Eternal Beauty.

No thinking about religion, particularly if it is within the Christian tradition, can leave out all consideration of faith. 'It has not pleased the Lord to save his people by dialectic', and no philosophy of religion, however well thought out, is equivalent to a religious belief in God. The reliance upon faith has been represented by sceptics such as Hume as implying that Christianity is irrational. The tacit assumption here is that faith and reason are two distinct and inconsistent states of mind. This is clearly a mistake, because men of faith are frequently acute reasoners and are ready to defend their faith by rational arguments. The inquiry into the nature of faith and its relation with reason would take us into a wide field and we must limit ourselves to a brief statement of certain theses, which may at least direct reflection on to the salient points. First, it is instructive to observe that the word 'faith' in the New Testament has no defined meaning. There are variations of emphasis from one writer to another, and the idea of faith, for example, in St. Paul's Epistles is not precisely the same as that of St. John. Secondly, faith always has an intellectual element; it always includes belief, or the assent to some proposition or propositions; but, at the same time, faith is never only belief in the sense of assent. No-one would think of calling my conviction that William the Conqueror won the battle of Hastings an act of faith. Thirdly, it is a mistake to suppose that faith is only required in religion. So far is this from being true that all human activities are possible only by some kind of faith, including our day-to-day existence, with its reliance on the order of nature, on the stability of our society and the trustworthiness of our friends. Science itself is a great adventure of faith, of faith in the intelligibility of nature, a faith which is held often in the face of appearances to the contrary. Fourthly, faith appears to be an attitude of confidence towards life and reality, the kind of confidence which can lead to heroic action and endurance.

If these theses are accepted, we may go on to describe a little more closely the nature of religious faith. It is distinguished from reason, in the narrower sense of that word, by being an activity of the whole personality, in which feeling, imagination and will are involved and not the activity of the intellect alone. The difference can be illustrated from our relation with other persons. I may know very much about another person without trusting him or believing in him. When I come to the point of trust and belief my affections and will are engaged. I have a personal relation with him: I respond with my whole self to him.

Every kind of faith, we may say, is a personal response to some side or aspect of the real world. Living is always responding: and living on the level of self-consciousness is a continual response of the self to the environment. Religious faith is the response of the whole personality to the values which are as real as the physical objects which surround us—perhaps indeed more real. Or, to put the matter in plain words, it is the response of the person as a whole to the divine environment. Faith in

c

God is the response of the human spirit to the divine Spirit, and faith in Christ is the response to the divine manifested in human life.

At the end, we come to a paradox, which is the sign that we have reached the limit of the scope of our understanding. The paradox is this: We have to think for ourselves and employ our own reason; we have to believe and have faith for ourselves, for we cannot live by another's faith. We are, it appears, responsible for our reasoning and our faith; and yet, if we believe in God, we must also believe that every good gift comes from him, that our power to reason is dependent on his will and our faith is not our own achievement but the working of God's grace.

PART I

GOD AND THE WORLD

Science and Religion

Henry Balmforth

THE field of science is so vast and contains such a multitude of different studies that no one, not even professional scientists themselves, can today give a balanced, comprehensive account of it. But the several sciences have a certain common character. They share a common outlook and method. I am not a professional scientist, but I have tried for many years to understand the scientific outlook and scientific method. In such a position, I ask those of my readers who are, or aspire to be, scientists by training, or whose business perhaps it is to teach science, to excuse me if I have inadvertently misstated any matter of scientific fact. But we are not here and now concerned with the technical detail of the scientific worker; our business is with the general character of the scientific approach to truth and with its relationship to the religious interpretation of the world in which we find ourselves and of man's life and destiny. These are matters which concern everybody who is willing to think at all; consideration of them cannot be confined within the circle of professional scientists. The scientists will claim no exclusive rights here. Their right is to insist that we outside observers shall be careful about what we say on scientific subjects; and I shall do my utmost to respect that right and to say nothing for which I cannot produce competent scientific backing.

What is science? It is necessary to ask that question at the outset, because the answer is not obvious or easy. There are deep philosophical issues connected with it. We are brought face to face with them if we look at the descriptions of science given by two of the greatest scientists of this century. Here is Einstein's view: 'the object of all science is to co-ordinate our experiences and to bring them into a logical system'. And here is Bohr: 'the task of science is both to extend the range of our experience and to reduce it to order'.

We have to take seriously the stress laid by both of these accounts on human experience as the subject-matter of science. It is, perhaps, the most important feature of the modern scientific world-view, and the one which differentiates it from the world-view of the nineteenth-century scientists. The nineteenth century could still rely on the Newtonian mechanics and on the plain man's common-sense belief in an independently existing external universe of matter in motion, a universe easily visualized, in three dimensions, theoretically capable of being mapped and described by any competent observer with sufficient knowledge. Now the picture is very different. Instead of the old spatial structure of molecules, causally linked in a single closed system, fundamentally simple despite the immense variety of the things which make up the order of Nature, we have the mysterious space-time continuum of relativity theory. This awe-inspiring affair can be described only with reference to the observer and, even then, only in a set of equations which the mathematical expert may, and no one else can, comprehend.

From this demise of the 'billiard-ball universe' many important results follow. The exponents of relativity theory tell us that the scientist's observations of his subject-matter are unavoidably relative to the observer. Hence he does not approach his work as the passive recorder of an externally existing system which causes him to have certain experiences; his business is with the experiences themselves and with experiences in which he is actor as well as observer. It is these which he endeavours to co-ordinate, as Einstein puts it, and to bring into a logical system.

For this purpose the contemporary scientist is ready to use whatever co-ordinating hypotheses he finds convenient, though this procedure may land him in apparent paradox.

If for different purposes different hypotheses fit best, he will use them whether or not they are mutually compatible. Thus, we are told, four different hypotheses are appropriate to different groups of phenomena—those of Newton, Riemann, Einstein and Planck; but they are mutually incompatible and even irreconcilable. In quantum-theory, according to Niels Bohr, the speed and the location of a particle are 'complementary'. This means that you can focus on one or the other, but not on both; now one, now the other can be described, but the two kinds of description will not admit of reconciliation in a wider generalized formula.

If follows, too, that the so-called Laws of Nature must be reconsidered. They must be recognized as no more than statistical averages, not as inflexible rules governing any and every thing that exists. The old rigid determinism gives way to complementarity and to Heisenberg's 'uncertainty' principle, when we come to the underlying atomic structure of matter.

Again, if 'experience' is the subject-matter of science, then the older dominance of physics and chemistry as normative, as, so to speak, the sources and standards of all truly scientific information, has to be reconsidered. It becomes difficult to deny the title of science to psychology, including psychical research or para-psychology, to anthropology and to the social sciences generally. For mental phenomena are just as much parts of human experience as are the physical phenomena of light and heat or the chemical phenomena of inorganic and organic compounds. It is no longer necessary for scientific respectability that what is studied should be weighed in a chemical balance or measured on a scale.

In these and other ways there has been a notable 'loosening-up' in the scientific outlook. From one point of view it may appear as an invasion of scepticism, when we find scientific writers rejecting the idea of an independent, objective order of Nature and laying much stress on the human limitations of scientific knowing, despite the astonishing variety and range of the concrete operations which applied science can bring off. But from another point of view we may welcome the departure of that over-simplified, over-confident version of this mysterious universe which seemed to imply that one day it would be possible to give a complete 'explanation' of *Romeo and Juliet* by means of Newton's mechanics. Science today is a much more flexible, open-minded and adaptable affair.

This 'new look' in contemporary science suggests a further gain. As I see it, it frees us from the tyrannous convention which limited all genuine knowledge of truth to that which could be tested in the laboratory and given mathematical expression. For myself, I venture to think that it is a great pity that the word 'science' should ever have been narrowed into meaning only that kind of knowing which is attained by laboratory procedures. Science, etymologically, is *scientia*, knowing or knowledge; and there are vast fields of knowledge, vitally important for human beings, which cannot be submitted to laboratory tests. Only a radical and quite arbitrary scepticism or irrational prejudice can deny them the name of knowledge. The scientific procedures of observation, analysis and verification can be and are applied on levels of human experience quite other than those of the laboratory. And there are wide areas of human knowing, notably that of history, in which knowledge can and does exist without direct observation and direct experimental verification of the matters known.

The knowledge we have of other people is perhaps the crucial case. We may, of course, 'know' other people by the scientific procedures of the anthropological research worker, yearning for a Ph.D., or by the tortuous manoeuvres of Her Majesty's Inspector of Taxes delving into our private affairs for his own professional purposes. But our knowing of people is far wider than that. Our families and friends are known to us with a certainty that cannot be denied without manifest absurdity. The knowledge is never complete—no knowledge is. It is not exempt from error and delusion—no knowledge is. But it is genuine knowing; and on the basis of that knowing far the greater parts of our lives are organized. For the most valuable things in life we depend upon it—family relationships, friendships, all those personal bonds which make life properly human for all of us, scientists included. Socrates and Plato, St. Paul and St. Augustine, Virgil and Dante lived before the age of modern science and they lived fully and nobly human lives, guided by knowledge of truth.

This is, of course, in no way to depreciate scientific knowledge in the narrower sense. This knowledge has added immeasurably to the accuracy and range of our understanding of the world we live in and of ourselves and other people. It has done wonders innumerable in the relief of human suffering and the enrichment of human experience. Scientific knowledge corrects and extends all our apprehension of truth and reality.

How does it do this? It has often been alleged that scientific truth is the only truth because its strictly empirical and rational procedures in the investigation of truth are free from all the distortions which come in from reliance on authority and dependence upon faith. Thus we used to be told that religious doctrines were alien to the scientifically trained mind because they rested upon faith and authority, not on reason and experimental verification. But this seems to me to misrepresent both science and religion. Science itself cannot get on without faith and authority. Religion, at least the historic Christian religion, has said ever since the days of St. Augustine, 'I believe in order that I may understand', and has laid great stress on verification in life of doctrines accepted by the mind as true.

It is not difficult to see that faith and authority have their place in science. All scientific inquiry rests upon an unproved and unprovable assumption, an act of faith. For in exploring any new field of research the scientist assumes that it will turn out to be amenable to those scientific procedures which he will use upon it. He does not know that it will be so, nor has he verified his assumption in this case. Again, in applying his knowledge of his subject-matter, he has constantly to assume that what has proved in the past to be the behaviour of the stuff he is handling will continue to be its behaviour in the future. But he does not know that it will be so; he has no experimental proof that it will be so. Water boils at a certain temperature at a certain pressure; we cannot possibly know that it will continue to do so in the future. We risk it; we gamble on it, if you like. We certainly make an act of faith. The fact that water has behaved so in the past gives us no logical certainty, only a psychological presumption, that the future will be exactly conformable to our past experience. The construction and use of steam engines would be quite impossible and quite irrational without that act of faith.

Authority, too, comes in. I remember a physicist friend of mine once telling me, with a fierce gleam in his eye, that the only authority he accepted was the authority of the experimental facts. Well, you know, it will not do. No living scientist has ever performed or ever could perform, for himself, all the experiments upon which his science rests. For the greater part of his knowledge he takes the word of those who are his teachers, his authorities. He could perhaps himself perform any one of the crucial experiments for himself, and that would be a test case. But what of all the other experiments? In fact, his test case would go to strengthen still further his reliance upon the authority that had been subjected to the test and justified by it.

I am not saying that the faith and authority we find in science are precisely the same as the faith and authority we find in the Christian religion. There are differentials here, due to the differences in the subject-matter. Belief in God or in the resurrection of Jesus Christ from the dead is obviously not exactly on the same level as the scientist's belief that if next Tuesday he passes an electric current through a mixture of hydrogen and oxygen he will get water. My only point now is that there is no unbridgeable gulf, no absolute disparity between scientific truth and the truths we apprehend outside the borders of what we call 'the sciences'. When, for example, religion leaves room for authority and faith as well as for reason in its approach to the historical fact of Jesus Christ, it is not being blindly obscurantist or irrational or superstitious in doing so. It is doing something which our human knowing generally is found to do, and indeed is bound to do in some measure, whenever we seek to reach truth. Reason and faith are not irreconcilable enemies. They are partners in a common quest.

I have mentioned the historical fact of Jesus Christ and it is time to turn now from the question, What is science? to the question, What is religion? I hold no brief for religion in general, whatever that commodity may be. I shall speak from within the framework of that historic faith which has emerged from the coming of Jesus Christ and is sufficiently stated in the Apostles' Creed and the Nicene Creed. This religion rests upon a divine revelation recorded in the Bible. That biblical revelation includes doctrines about creation, about the nature of man, about divine providence and judgement and mercy manifested in historical events, some of them miraculous. It culminates in the life, death and resurrection of Jesus Christ and the inauguration of a new order of human existence in the Church, beginning here on earth and continuing, on a different level, in the resurrection life after physical death. What has this religion to say about science, and what has science to say about it?

I cannot here survey the chequered history of the relations between scientists and ecclesiastics since the Middle Ages. It is a long, complicated story and there are many controversial points in it. I will just say that, as we all know, ever since the days of Copernicus (to go no further back) there has been a long-drawn debate with varying shifts of ground by both parties. If we take the seventeenth century as the period when modern science got into its stride, we have had 300 years in which new knowledge has accumulated with such astonishing rapidity that it is no wonder that the process of assimilation has been a strain and has not infrequently produced symptoms of acute mental dyspepsia. Theologians have defended the indefensible, because they were working with wrong or inadequate ideas of the meaning of Scripture. Scientists have made rash incursions into philosophical territory with insufficient equipment. A recent example will perhaps be fresh in the reader's mind: that of a distinguished astrophysicist whose brilliance in his own field was only equalled by his astonishing incompetence when he embarked upon the unfamiliar seas of theology.

If we try to learn the lessons of this not always edifying and frequently boring controversy and use them, with honesty and humility of mind, when we reflect upon the relations between science and religion in our own day, we may perhaps be able to paint a less distorted picture of that relationship than our fathers could. Let me then devote the remaining part of this chapter to a brief consideration of some of the points at which the scientific and the Christian world-views overlap and may be mutually helpful.

First, we may take the topical question of creation and scientific cosmology. The essential Christian affirmation is that the material universe is created by God and is not an independent entity. The process of creation has to be distinguished from this fact of the ultimate dependence of the created universe upon God. It is for human reason to discover, if it can, in what ways and by what stages the divine creativity proceeds; and in that discovery scientific investigation is obviously of primary importance. The creation stories at the beginning of the Bible are not to be understood as substitutes for this investigation. They are not concerned to state the astronomical, geological and biological history of our planet, but to affirm the theological truth of creatureliness, that fundamental truth about things, namely, that, whatever else may be true of them, they are the creatures of God. It should be obvious from the pictorial and imaginative character of the biblical narratives that they are stating this theological truth in the language of symbolism: a procedure which is wholly appropriate to the kind of knowledge which they convey. For only in the language of symbol can we express what lies, and must lie, beyond the observable data of experience.

I think it is not too much to say that the Church is committed to no particular cosmology, but can utilize any cosmology that sticks to its business of describing process and does not go beyond its proper scientific purpose into metaphysical denials of the dependence of the material universe upon the creative will of God. Actually, we have no one theory upon which all scientific cosmologists are agreed and the problem is still unsolved. What we do know more about today than the ancient world knew is the immense size of the universe. The idea is, indeed, not new. On this subject I like to recall one of the Fathers of the Church who, writing in the fourth century, found much to edify him in the thought of man's littleness by comparison with the vast range of God's creation. Yet it is sometimes supposed that the knowledge which makes the earth a minor planet, attached to a comparatively small star among millions of other stars, reduces man to complete insignificance and incidentally makes his religious ideas either ludicrous or pathetic, according to taste.

But this is a mere confusion of thought. It brings everything down to the quantitative level and then begs the whole question by assuming that only quantitative reckoning is relevant. And it is self-contradictory, because it then proceeds to use qualitative terms and makes judgments of value about significance. The truth is that, when the human mind shows itself capable of considering and describing the measureless size of the universe, that is a far more revealing and important fact than man's quantitative smallness; unless indeed we assume that mind does not matter!

The sciences of anthropology and psychology provide further illustrations of the need to distinguish between the proper field of scientific inquiry and those theological evaluations of man which emerge from his relation to God. That man, as a biological species, has descended in the process of evolution from non-human ancestors is highly probable; and it is difficult for us today to see why anyone should ever have been disturbed by this idea. The idea, in fact, though not the evidence for it, is a very ancient one. We may perhaps add that the picturesque metaphor of the book of Genesis, according to which man was made of the dust of the earth, might seem to give him an even humbler origin, and one more derogatory to his dignity. As, however, man now indubitably exists as man and has certain powers of intelligence and will that mark him off decisively from all other terrestrial animals, the stages by which he reached humanity are not the whole story of man. Similarly, the mechanisms of his psychological activity are not the whole story of his mind, which cannot be sufficiently accounted for by precarious theories of instincts inherited from his pre-human ancestry. Man does not only seek food and propagate his kind. He builds cathedrals, writes symphonies, constructs scientific and philosophical systems, and, more than all this, he can seek after and worship God.

If, as Christianity holds, man is the creature of God, made to know and love God in his own characteristically human fashion—as an embodied soul, that is; if he is one with the rest of Nature and yet capable of transcending his material environment by his intellectual and spiritual powers; if that is so, then science and religious faith are both necessary. Science will tell him the story of his past and of the raw material of his bodily and psychical make-up; but religion will have to tell him what it is all for, to what end he is to organize his remarkable and wonderful powers.

I have already referred to the theory of evolution; and the dovetailing of scientific knowledge into the framework of theological understanding will again be apparent, if we consider a little further the theory of evolution in relation to the doctrine of divine creation.

Science, which deals with experience, with process and observable data, can throw much light on the evolution of living organisms and the way the process works. But why it works, why it exists at all, are questions which we still have to ask. If reason and revelation combine to tell us of a creative will as the ultimate answer to these questions, then evolution will appear as the method of creation in the biological order. The biblical revelation neither asserts nor denies an evolutionary process in creation. It is not concerned with that kind of thing, but, as I said earlier, with the theological interpretation of existing things as the creatures of God. What does seem to be impossible is to make evolution a substitute for God. Evolution is not a force or a living agent; it is an abstract noun, by which we summarize a vast multitude of detailed changes and co-ordinate them in a systematic pattern. The discovery of an Order may suggest an Orderer, a constructive mind which is intelligent and purposive, even though many of its workings may baffle lower intelligences such as ours. But it is mere muddle-headedness to say that this Orderer *is* evolution.

It is in connexion with this idea of an Order of Nature that we are confronted by what is for the scientific mind one of the most difficult elements in Christianity: I mean the miraculous element. It is, I suppose, inevitable that the scientist should regard the miraculous as something foreign to his whole outlook. For him it must be just the unexplained or misunderstood, because his scientific impulse is, first, to discover how things behave, and then to see the patterns, the ordered sequences, into which that behaviour falls. To admit the miraculous is, it would seem, to admit disorder, and so the exclusion of science from some areas of experience. And he is fortified in his rejection of miracles by the many successes of science in providing natural explanations for what had previously been accounted preternatural occurrences.

Here, I think, we must make a distinction between the historical and the philosophical issues involved. This is not an essay in scriptural exegesis and I am not now concerned with the miracles actually recorded in the Bible. I shall say nothing about them except that I can see no reason why an orthodox Christian should feel himself bound to defend the literal historicity of every miracle-story in Scripture. Christian orthodoxy does not depend upon fundamentalist ideas about Holy Scripture. What we are concerned with now is something different, namely, whether miracles as such are to be ruled out as incompatible with any rational account of the nature of things.

In my view, any theistic interpretation of existence, and Christian theism in particular, is bound to say that they are not incompatible. For if we are theists, we are asserting the transcendence and sovereignty of God over the created order; and we are logically required to infer from that transcendence that God is not bound by the norms which he has established in the sequences of nature. He may, and for certain special purposes we should expect that he will, modify those sequences by his sovereign authority.

Miracles will be rare and exceptional; otherwise they would not be miracles. Yet there is nothing in the nature of things to prevent their occurrence in any circumstances whatsoever. The miraculous is simply one possible outcome of that divine transcendence which is essential to theism as distinct from any pantheistic doctrine of the universe. It will elude the scientist just because the scientist is concerned with the norms, the regular sequences which make up the every-day working of the universe. He excludes the miraculous from his science, not because the miraculous cannot happen, but because by a self-denying ordinance he has left it out of the subject-matter of his study.

Hence it is of no avail to seek a supposed scientific explanation of the two crucial miracles which have been included in the official creeds of the Church: the virgin birth of the Lord and his resurrection from the dead. We are not concerned with an unusual case of animal parthenogenesis or with the mere revival of a dead body. We are concerned with wholly unique and mysterious and exceptional acts of God, which are related to, and congruous with, the wholly unique and exceptional act of the Incarnation of the Word of God; something that could, in the nature of the case, happen only once. I believe, as historic Christianity has always believed, that these acts did occur; but that is not the point I am now making. My point is that we should be quite clear what it is that we are talking about: namely, that the abnormality of these events is no reason why, in the interests of the scientific study of Nature, we should veto them outright. In this matter, I would maintain, we can be perfectly good scientists and perfectly orthodox Christians.

In this brief chapter I have tried to deal with some aspects of a very large and difficult subject and to suggest certain lines of thought. And the treatment of what I have touched upon has of necessity been very sketchy. If we were to attempt any complete survey—a survey impossible in a single chapter—there is much more that we should have to consider, of which I have said nothing

D

at all. For example, I have left entirely out of account the moral issues raised by the technological applications of scientific knowledge: such matters as the manufacture of atom and hydrogen bombs, or again eugenics, euthanasia, the sterilization of the unfit, or certain operations on the brain. I have this excuse for leaving aside these matters of the gravest importance: they all concern the *use* of scientific knowledge, not the prime objective of science, which is the acquiring of knowledge. The scientist, *qua* scientist, is not responsible for the uses made of his discoveries by other people. We cannot restrict scientific inquiry merely on the ground that the results may be used in morally bad or doubtful ways. Nuclear fission, which can have the most horrible results, can also be turned to socially useful ends, and apparently will be so turned before we are very much older, and that on an immense scale.

Leaving this aside, then, what shall we say in conclusion about the relation between religion and the scientific knowledge of today?

It will have been apparent from what I have said already that I do not see any ultimate incompatibility between the two. I have never heard of any actual piece of scientific discovery or of any body of scientific knowledge that makes it intellectually impossible or even difficult to hold the Christian faith. It is true that philosophical theories have been constructed out of material drawn from the sciences and that some of them, like dialectical materialism, are avowedly atheist: 'there is no god and Karl Marx is his prophet'. And there are other theories, like Freud's, which make the idea of God not merely untrue but positively bad for the nerves. But it is not science that tells the Marxian or the Freudian that he is right. It is the history not of scientific discovery but of philosophy, that tells us how Marxian atheism emerges from the old impossibly crude materialism by way of Hegel's dialectic. And the Freudian theory tells us nothing about God, but only about the queer religious notions that appear in certain kinds of psychoneurotic illness. We do not need Freud to inform us that religion is not always a good thing. We have known for a very long time that it can be positively evil, a worship of false gods of many kinds. We learnt it, or should have learnt it, from the Bible, which is full of warnings against this very thing.

Science, real science, is profoundly religious because it seeks truth, as real religion does. But the apprehension of truth is on different levels and science does not enable us to apprehend truth on all levels. There is an apprehension of truth through the arts, which takes us beyond the truth of the sciences. Still more profound is the vision of truth seen in human love and self-sacrifice and heroism, that moral beauty which is so compelling and so illuminating. So too, on the deepest level of all, there is the truth about God and man revealed in Jesus Christ. This takes us deeper than either science or art or even human love, because it shows us those ultimates which give to scientific inquiry and artistic creation and self-sacrificing love their place and meaning in the nature of things. For these human concerns are seen to be, not the pathetic illusions of a being who is only the chance product of a meaningless whirl of hydrogen atoms, but the richly meaningful activities of a creature of God; a creature whose final end is to know and love God, and in that knowledge and love to reach the fulfilment of his being and his endless beatitude.

The Biblical Story of Creation and Modern Science

S. H. HOOKE

THE first article in the Nicene Creed is a confession of faith in one God, the Father, Almighty, Maker of heaven and earth and of all things visible and invisible. To this every believing Jew would give assent, for it rests upon statements in the Jewish scriptures, which we call the Old Testament. But when we come to examine the Old Testament to see what it has to say about creation, we find that it is somewhat misleading to speak about the biblical story of creation, since the Old Testament contains several accounts or descriptions of the divine act which we call creation. These accounts come from different periods of the religious history of Israel, were written by different people, and have each a different purpose in view, although they all agree in one essential respect in that they all acknowledge that creation is the act of a divine Person, the one God of Israel. We shall examine three of these accounts in order to see what the act or process of creation meant to Israel, and what sort of a universe they believed to have come into being as the result of the act of creation.

The first is found in the second chapter of Genesis and probably represents the earliest picture of creation as it was conceived in the minds of the ancestors of the Hebrew people. It begins in the middle of verse 4 with the words, 'In the day that the Lord God made earth and heaven no plant of the field was yet in the earth, and no herb of the field had yet sprung up'. The original state of the universe in which the divine activity began to operate was a waterless waste without vegetation of any kind, and man did not yet exist. The first thing that happened, whether by a divine act or not is left undetermined, was the upspringing, from underground sources, of moisture which prepared the ground for the growth of vegetation. The word in verse 6 rendered 'mist' is of uncertain meaning, but is usually interpreted to mean the coming up of springs from the waters under the earth. The first divine act is the creation of man. It says, 'The Lord God formed man of the dust of the ground, and breathed into his nostrils the breath of life; and man became a living soul.' The word 'formed', which is used to describe the divine act, is the word commonly used in Hebrew for the potter's work. The dust is kneaded with moisture into clay, and the clay figure is quickened into life by the inbreathing of the breath of God. The remaining acts in their order are, the planting of a garden in Eden, in which man is placed; trees of every kind are caused to grow out of the ground, including the tree of life and the tree of the knowledge of good and evil; beasts and birds are 'formed' out of the ground; and lastly woman is 'built' out of a rib taken from the man's side. Although this is the only part of the story which concerns us here, it must be pointed out that it cannot be separated from what follows, the story 'Of man's first disobedience and the fruit Of that forbidden tree whose mortal taste Brought death into the world, and all our woe.'

There are several things to be noted about this origin-story. First, there is no thought here of a creation *ex nihilo*; that was a conception which was foreign to the mind of the ancient world. The process of creation consisted in bringing order out of chaos, and in this particular form of the tradition the primitive state of things was a waterless waste, devoid of any kind of life. Secondly, the centre of interest is man; he is the first created being, he is differentiated from the animals by having the divine breath as the source of his life, and the development of the story is intended to furnish an explanation of the existence of various elements in human experience, the presence of death, the pains of childbirth, the necessity of tilling the soil to gain a living, and the dim sense of something lost. Thirdly, the story contains the implication that the knowledge of good and evil was something which man had obtained by unlawful means, and yet that the possession of it had in some way made him like God, 'Behold, the man is become as one of us, to know good and evil'.

The second form of the Hebrew tradition of creation is contained in the first chapter of Genesis and ends in the middle of verse 4 of chapter 2 with the words, 'These are the generations of the heaven and of the earth when they were created'. This section of Genesis is of much later date than the part which we have just been considering, and is not an explanatory origin-story but liturgical in form, and may perhaps have been sung at the Hebrew New Year festival by the priests. Its possible liturgical use is suggested by the regular recurrence of the refrain, 'And God saw that it was good. And there was evening and there was morning, day one, . . . two, etc.' This suggestion is supported by the fact that the Babylonian Epic of Creation, which has marked affinities with our passage, was chanted by the priests at the New Year Festival.

In this form of the tradition the original state of the universe before the creative activity began was chaos, a waste of waters and darkness. There is some doubt whether the words rendered by the R.V. 'the spirit of God moved upon the face of the waters', refer to divine action. They can be quite correctly rendered, as in Goodspeed's translation, 'a tempestuous wind raging over the surface of the waters'; in which case the phrase will simply add a detail to the picture of chaos, and might be compared with Daniel 7 : 2, 'The four winds of heaven brake forth upon the great sea'.

The stages of the divine activity in creation are then divided into six periods, called 'days', followed by a seventh day of rest. The stages are: first day, creation of light and division of light from darkness; second day, creation of a solid vault or expanse, called Heaven, dividing the waters above from the waters below; third day, separation of the dry land, called Earth, from the seas, and the creation of vegetation; fourth day, creation of the heavenly bodies; fifth day, creation of fishes and birds; sixth day, creation of animals, and finally of man, male and female, in 'the image of God'. On the seventh day God rests and blesses the day on which he had finished his work of creation.

The differences between this account of creation and the earlier are obvious. In the first place the original state of things is not a waterless waste, but a chaos of storm-tossed waters; the process of creation is much more clearly seen to be the bringing of order out of chaos; in the earlier account the scene of the divine activity is a garden, in the later it is the whole universe as the Hebrew mind conceived of it; in the earlier account man is created first, and woman separately as an after-thought, while in the later, man, male and female, is the crown of God's creative activity, created last of all, in the divine image.

The third picture of creation, probably the latest of the three, is a poet's picture. It is taken from the thirty-eighth chapter of the book of Job and contains some of the finest poetry in Hebrew literature. The poet represents God as confronting Job with the majestic panorama of his creative acts. He begins with the laying of the foundations of the earth, the stretching of the measuring-line over it, the placing of its pillars on their sockets, and the laying of its cornerstone, 'when the morning stars sang together, and all the sons of God shouted for joy'. It goes on to describe the creation of light, and the place of darkness, and the underworld; the ordering of the heavenly bodies, and all the divine providential care for the whole animal creation. We have similar poetic descriptions of God's creative activity in the various psalms and in 'Second Isaiah', but they all present the same picture of Hebrew cosmogony, and of the divine activity which brought it into being. Neither of the first two accounts gives such a clear picture of how the Hebrew mind conceived of the material universe as the poet's images do.

Hence it will be seen how impossible it is to speak of the biblical story of creation as if we possessed one continuous and coherent narrative of how the world was made. The three examples which we have selected from Hebrew literature of various periods will suffice to show the different ways in which Hebrew writers approached the subject of how their world began. In spite of the striking differences between them, they all have this in common, that for them the essential truth is, in the words of the nineteenth psalm, 'the heavens declare the glory of God, and the firmament showeth his handi-work'. The problems which occupied the mind of the Hebrew thinker were moral problems. He was not inter-ested, as the early Ionian physicists were, in the nature and origin of the material universe, but in what the universe could tell him about the nature of God and his ways with man. The book of Genesis in the form in which we have it now is the final result of the literary and editorial activity of deeply religious men who were concerned to preserve all the ancient traditions of their people in a form which would make these traditions the vehicle of their beliefs about God and his purpose for Israel. They lived and wrote at a time when Israel was no longer an independent political entity, but an unim-portant subject of a great heathen empire, the Persian. Hence the material in the book of Genesis represents at the same time both the earliest and the latest stages of the religious development of Israel. There are elements in the stories contained in the first eleven chapters of Genesis which show their undoubted relation to the myths of Babylon and Egypt, and, as we now know, to those of Canaan. These elements are too well known to need repeating here. But the same material also shows the way in which it has been transformed by passing through the minds of men who believed that everything began with God, one God, holy, righteous, and almighty, whose purpose of blessing for man gave meaning to all the past history of their people as they knew it from their traditions, oral or written.

It is a mistaken view of what the Bible is that has led people to suppose that the ancient traditions of the Hebrew people collected in the early chapters of Genesis are historical truth. Although this was the accepted belief of the Christian Church for many centuries, and even still survives in some quarters, yet as early as the third century A.D. a great Christian scholar could write: 'What man of any intelligence can suppose that there was a first, a second, and a third day, evening and morning, at a time when there was no sun or moon or stars? Nay, that a "first" day could have been, when as yet there was no "heaven"? Who can be so foolish as to suppose that God "planted a garden eastward in Eden", as if he were a human worker on the land; that God made to grow in the garden a visible and material "tree of life", of a such a sort that men might acquire life by eating its fruit with their literal bodily teeth? Or again, that they could come to understand "good and evil" by literally chewing the fruit of this other tree?' (Origen, *De Principiis* iv. 3.)

The question then naturally arises, If these stories do not possess historical truth, what is their value, and why are they found in a book which is regarded as having divine authority? In answer to this question three things may be said: first, they are of great value as showing that the ancestors of the Hebrew people shared in the common stock of myths concerning the origin of the ordered world in which they lived; second, they are of even greater value as bearing witness to the way in which the prophets' experience of God had power to transform the ancient myths of origin into a magnificent assertion of the divine activity, that all things had their source of being in the one eternal and unchanging God; thirdly, their greatest value is revealed when we consider them in relation to the whole revelation of God in Christ. They are then seen to be a storehouse of living images and symbols, an indispensable part of the divine speech by which things can be said about God and his ways which could not be said in any other way. The garden, the tree, the serpent, even the far-off myth of the fight between Marduk and the chaos-dragon Tiamat, still preserved in Hebrew poetry, all become images of realities which in the end find their full meaning and expression in Christ.

We must now turn from the biblical accounts of creation and examine what modern science has to say about the origin of the universe and man. There is a tendency today to write science with a capital, almost to personify it, and set it up as an authority against the Bible. But to believe uncritically in the infallibility of modern science is just as foolish and just as dangerous as to believe in the infallibility of the Bible. As we have seen, what the Bible has to say about the origin of things is not an authoritative statement about how the universe came into existence, but a record of what Hebrew poets and prophets thought and believed about God's activity in creation. Their description of his activity is couched in language and in images partly drawn from ancient tradition and more largely based on religious experience, but belonging wholly to a conception of the universe which has ceased to have the force of literal truth for us today. Similarly what science has to say about the origin of the universe is not a single, unambiguous, authoritative statement about how our material world came into being, nor is there any such entity as Science with a big S. Science is simply human knowledge. That somewhat misleading term embraces all the results of patient and careful work in many fields of research. Science is not one, but manifold: there is geology, there is chemistry, there are the various branches of physics, especially noteworthy being astrophysics; there is biology and bio-chemistry; time would fail me, as said the writer of the Epistle of the Hebrews, if I were to attempt to enumer-ate all the fresh fields of knowledge which the human mind is ever opening up as it explores the endless mystery of the universe. Anyone who cares to read such books as *The Idea of Nature* by the late Professor R. G. Collingwood, or Professor Butterfield's *The Origins of Modern Science*, may discover how far from infallible are the findings of the long process of exploration that began with the Ionian physicists and still continues with unabated energy. It is a record of false starts, mistaken guesses, and erroneous inferences based on insufficient data. But it is also a record of gradual consolidation of new knowledge, of conquest of the unknown by the help of improved instruments and new techniques; and what is specially significant is that the record shows a resolute discarding of past errors, and an unshakable determin-ation to test every hypothesis, together with the faith to frame fresh hypotheses when fresh data showed the old hypotheses to be no longer tenable.

But what we are concerned with at present is the question of what modern science, defined as above, has to say about the origin of the material universe and more especially about the origin of man as a spiritual being. Here it may be relevant to quote a passage from Profes-sor A. N. Whitehead, *Adventures of Ideas*, p. 198: 'Our co-ordinated knowledge, which in the general sense of the term is Science, is formed by the meeting of two orders of experience. One order is constituted by the direct, immediate discriminations of particular observa-tions. The other order is constituted by our general way of conceiving the universe.' He goes on to point out that the observational order is always interpreted in terms of the concepts supplied by the conceptual order. In the history of the development of human knowledge we can see that the range of observed facts has enormously increased since the Hebrew writers wrote about the event which they called creation, and we can also see that this increased range of observation has completely transformed the conceptual order which underlies the Hebrew accounts of creation. It is true that, as Whitehead points out, there is a serious weakness in the observational order, namely, a tendency to distort observed facts by selecting and arranging them in a subjective order of prominence. Nevertheless, the ultimate foundation of modern science is observation of facts, and all hypotheses must abide the test of observed facts. Now, with regard to the fact or event implied by the term 'creation', modern science, pursuing its course of observing facts, has never reached the stage of being able to say that at this or that definite point of space-time a pattern of events has been observed to which the name 'creation' can be given. Indeed, creation, by its very meaning, lies outside the observational order altogether. We cannot imagine man observing his own creation, or that of the physical universe. Quite apart from the religious issue, the idea of creation belongs to what Whitehead has called the conceptual order; it is based on the common experience that everything seems to have a beginning or a maker. But, as we have seen, the vastly increased range and complexity of observation due to the advance of science has completely transformed the way in which we now conceive of the universe; indeed, at the present moment, as the result of the revolutionary findings of nuclear physics, our whole conception of the physical universe is undergoing a startling change. Just as the development of mathematics ultimately broke down the medieval cosmology, and led to the closed system of Newtonian physics, from which was born the purely mechanistic conception of the universe which dominated the nineteenth century, and still lingers in uninformed quarters, so the Newtonian universe has broken down before the wave-theory of matter and modern nuclear physics. It would be beyond my competence and the limits of this article to describe in detail the grounds upon which this changed view of the universe rests. A valuable account of its implications may be found in Karl Heim's book, *The Transformation of the Scientific World-View* (S.C.M. Press, 1953).

The most important result of this far-reaching change for our present inquiry is this. The acceptance, which characterized the nineteenth century, of a completely determined, mechanistic universe, left no room for any action upon such a universe *ab extra*, nor any room for indeterminateness. But the acceptance of the new quantum-mechanics rules out a deterministic sub-structure. 'Here therefore there remains room for happenings of the kind which have been called a-causal decisions' (Heim, op. cit. p. 136). Hence with the disappearance of Newton's absolute object, absolute time-space, and absolute causal determination, the universe is, so to speak, thrown open, it is expanding, and the possibilities of what theology calls divine action, either in the past, present, or future, can no longer be ruled out *a priori*.

Before bringing this discussion to a close, let us try to summarize the principal differences which appear when we compare the Hebrew world-view as implied in their pictures of creation with the modern conception of the universe as it presents itself to the scientist today. The Hebrew conception of the universe, like the medieval view which derived from it, was geocentric. The earth was the centre round which the sun, moon, and planets revolved. It was flat, surmounted by a solid arch of sky which sustained and held back an upper ocean; it was supported on pillars above an underworld ocean, and somewhere in the underworld was the place where the shades of dead persons had their gloomy abode. Above the solid vault, or firmament, were various heavens, peopled by celestial beings, and in the uppermost heaven was the throne and dwelling-place of God. The various forms of life, animal and vegetable, had been created in fixed types from which they could not depart. The conception of time, or change, was cyclic; the universe was moving in a great circle, to which Babylonian astrology assigned a definite number of years, back to the dissolution from which it had emerged. This, with slight change, remained the accepted view of the universe throughout the middle ages until in 1543 the revolutionary work of Copernicus on the solar system began the process of destruction of ancient and medieval cosmology.

The modern conception of the universe is so complex that it is difficult to summarize. Each of the various branches of science has made its own contribution towards the picture of a modern cosmology whose outlines are constantly changing from year to year. Geology has pushed back the age of the rocks which compose the earth's crust to an infinitely remote period, and together with organic chemistry, zoology and biology has enabled us to construct a picture of the gradual evolution of life on the planet from unicellular organisms up through monstrous creatures, known to us from their fossil remains, until the mammalian life of our own age is reached with *homo sapiens* as its latest product. Astronomy, building on the by no means negligible achievements of the Babylonian mathematicians and astrologers, has, with immensely more powerful instruments and vastly enhanced mathematical skill, explored the interstellar spaces and made us aware of its infinite distances peopled by innumerable planets, stars and nebulae, unknown to the ancients. Chemistry with the aid of the spectroscope has revealed the constituent elements of the heavenly bodies, and we even know the density of their atmospheres. But the crowning achievement of modern science has been the breaking up of what had seemed the irreducible atom of Newtonian physics into a dance of electrons, protons, and neutrons. With the discovery and accomplishment of nuclear fission man has acquired powers over the universe whose extent he is unable to measure and possibly unable to control. But there is one set of facts which science has hitherto been unable to explain or control, namely the facts of man's mental and spiritual life. The scientist who should venture to say today that the brain secretes mind as the liver secretes bile would be laughed out of court. Although the old antinomy of mind and matter has practically disappeared, the inner movements of man's spirit remain as mysterious as they ever were. Love, joy, hope, penitence, refuse to be reduced to an Oedipus-complex, or to an agitation of the nerve-centres, or to a deficiency of hormones. Biology can trace back the ancestry of man's physical structure to the amoeba, but it can tell us nothing about the origin of that fundamental difference between the most primitive savage and the most highly developed animal.

So, in the last resort, modern science can tell us a great deal about the nature of the universe, and, in the case of such scientists as Jeans, Eddington, or Whitehead, can see evidences of mind behind the universe, yet it can tell us nothing about how the dance of electrons began, nor about the origin of life. It has made unverifiable guesses about these problems, but it knows no more about them, that is to say about what we mean by creation, than did the author of the first chapter of Genesis. So, as Christians, while we gratefully accept all that science has disclosed to us of the wonders of the universe, we turn from them to God, and say with the writer to the Hebrews, 'By faith we understand that the worlds have been framed by the word of God, so that what is seen hath not been made out of things which do appear.' (Heb. 11: 3.)

E

God the Creator

C. A. COULSON

THE Christian religion claims to give an understanding to the whole of man's life and experience. The world in which we live is one element in that experience; so also are the sun, the moon and the stars. All these form part of everybody's first awareness of things and demand some sort of explanation. No wonder, then, that creation has always occupied a prominent part in Christian thinking. And by creation here I mean not just the bare outline of how this world, or any other possible worlds, came to be: but what we can discover from them; what meaning they have for us; how we can fit our understanding of them into our own personal experience of God, and the faith of the Church.

Our own Bible is full of creation. It begins with a statement about it—'In the beginning God created'— and it ends with an allegorical picture of a 'new creation'. There is hardly a psalm which does not speak of God's work in creation, and in practically all the official creeds of the Church, we make the affirmation—'I believe in God . . . maker of Heaven and Earth.'

The Christian faith would be quite impossible if we did not believe, in some form or other, that the world was made by God, to fulfil some pattern and some purpose of his. It is not merely that our actions are to be controlled and understood only by reference to him: it is also that the very stage on which our little act is to be performed, was designed by him. Not only does he direct the play; he actually built the theatre.

Now if this is so, we may quite legitimately reverse the argument. When we read a play, we can usually see something of the author in it: when we study the theatre, we may reasonably hope to see something of the Great Designer. God must, somehow, be revealed in his universe, if it is his at all: it is for man to explore him in it. And for us, reflecting on the nature of the physical world, it is the scientist who is the explorer. It ought to be part of the job of the scientist to show us what he sees of the nature of God. For the heavens, and not only the Bible, can declare the glory of God. We may—indeed we must—claim the help of the astronomer, the chemist, the anatomist and the geologist, in interpreting the ways of God to men; we ought not only to assert, but equally to make good our assertion, that—in words used as long ago as the thirteenth century, when science was just beginning to develop—one of the purposes of Natural Science was 'to assist the Church in her work of evangelizing mankind by leading the mind through scientific truth to the contemplation of the Creator'. I am going to 'jump a stage' in the argument, and say that I myself believe there are certain insights which are given to those of us who are professional scientists (just as, of course, there are other insights given to the artist, and the poet and the ordinary simple Christian) which are not given to anyone else, and without which, therefore, the total life of the Christian community is impoverished. That, incidentally, is why the scientist must be given complete and unqualified freedom to explore and experiment: that is why it is so important, in the name of holy living, that no theologian, or politician, or anybody else, should attempt in any way to impose restrictions on his work.

If what I have just been saying is correct, then the results of the scientists' researches are of greater importance than many of the scientists themselves realize, perhaps even more than we ourselves admit. It also follows that the quite unbelievable progress of science in the last three hundred years ought to be a cause of satisfaction to the Christian: and, of course, a continual challenge to us to discover its meaning and to relate it to our other experiences.

Let me, rather briefly and in non-technical terms, refer to three recent lines of scientific development. These three can do duty for all the others that could have been discussed. I choose these particular three because they are quite distinct from each other, and I shall come back to them again before I finish, when we try to interpret them within the Christian frontier. They concern physics, or perhaps better, astronomy, chemistry and anatomy.

First, then, astronomy. At the time when much of the Old Testament was being written, such as, e.g., the year 1000 B.C., when David was on the throne of Israel, 'considering the heavens' and drawing his own deductions about the status of man, current science supposed that the whole of the observable universe had sprung into existence at one instant of time, not really very far distant either: and that the stars represented windows cut out of the blue orb of the sky, each illuminated at night by a separate candle, so that the angels might more easily behold the doings of man. Even as late as 300 years ago, any educated man would have told you the date on which this planet came into existence a mere 5,600 years back, and he would have accepted substantially the story of Genesis as a literal description of the seven-day sequence of creation. It is almost unbelievable to think of the change that modern science has wrought in all this. No longer 'are we small boys at the holes of a circus tent, struggling to get even an imperfect peep at the great show, but we have ringside seats'. And it *is* a great show, dwarfing our imagination. Our sun is one among some hundred million others, all stars, that make our galaxy: our galaxy is one among some hundred million others that make our observable universe. And now we begin to trace the birth and death of the stars as their atmospheres of hydrogen are slowly consumed; and we picture the time when our own sun gets first steely blue, then orange, then red and finally takes its place among many others as a burnt out sphere, a black giant, a dull lump of lifeless matter. What if this process is to take fifty thousand million years? It hardly matters, for the show will go on, as other earths and other suns come into existence, 'strutting their little hour upon the stage, and then are heard no more'. Our own earth seems almost certain to be about three-and-a-half thousand million years old, a little less than the five thousand million years of the sun. As for its origin, if we look for the hand of God, we must find it, so many of the astronomers are now saying, in the immense holocaust which accompanied the explosion of a companion star to our sun, and left the planets as its legacy. Fred Hoyle, whose broadcast lectures many have either heard or read, was quite right when he said that 'Man's unguided imagination could never have chanced on such a structure. No literary genius could have invented a story one-hundredth part as fantastic as the sober facts unearthed by astronomical science.'

But I must pass on, and turn to chemistry. Some time ago I was involved in a small conference of people trying to discover the structure of one of our most recent vitamins, vitamin K. It is a complicated molecule, as you might suppose, and made up of four or five separate bits fastened together. Most of the details have now been worked out. But what struck me so vividly as I reflected on that discussion was the intricacy with which the whole thing was made. Here is something absolutely central to life, only needed in minute proportions and yet so sensitive that if, in a large molecule of a hundred atoms, one small change is made, its efficacy is entirely destroyed. This situation is not unique. There are certain chemicals which, if they are injected into an animal, will cause cancers. I have myself been interested to see if we can understand the mechanism of their action, and perhaps gain some clue to the greater problem, of cancer itself. Now here is the odd thing. If you alter one bit, and that one of the most inactive parts in other somewhat similar chemicals—then you destroy the cancer-producing property. It is as if the whole business of life was immensely more complicated than ever we had suspected before. When I was a boy, we used to hear about the wonders comprised within a single drop of water: those were nothing, absolutely nothing, compared with the astonishing discoveries of modern bio-chemistry.

Lastly, anatomy—and I am thinking more particularly of the brain. Recent research has shown that our brain consists of an almost innumerable set of nerve endings, joined by thin filaments capable of carrying tiny electric currents, and forming one gigantic network compared with which a London telephone exchange is a pin-prick. When we think, the rhythm of these circulating currents changes; when we are asleep, or when we are mad, the frequency and the pattern show it. The old gibe—that I can see you thinking—is now almost literally true. So magnificent have been the scientific developments along this line that it was possible for the B.B.C. Third Programme to run a complete series of talks, on 'the physical basis of mind'. The question which is raised by this, and (in their own way) by the two earlier fields of science, is a pretty insistent one—what do you make of it? Is there a revelation of God here? And if so, what is it? What, for example, has happened to the mind if thoughts are simply patterns of electric currents?

It is just there that we begin to run into difficulties. Fortunately it is the scientists themselves who have shown us most clearly the nature of the problem, and its solution. If we would try to find a revelation of God in science, it must not be, as it very often used to be, that we bring God in to explain what has so far baffled our scientists. That has often been done in the past, even by the great Isaac Newton himself, and it always ends in trouble. Let me illustrate what I mean. Newton once wrote in a letter: 'the diurnal rotations of the planets could not be derived from gravity, but required a divine hand to impress them.' Of course it was not long before a possible explanation of these rotations was found, and God became an unnecessary hypothesis. The doctrine— where science ends, there we may find God beginning— is quite fatal, despite its distinguished ancestry. Do you remember how Descartes had to locate the soul in the pineal gland because there seemed nowhere else for it? No wonder that scientists were soon abandoning the soul: it could not exist on these terms. Let me put it this way—God cannot be at the end of science, but at the beginning: not beyond science, but in it.

I think we can see this sort of thing better now—thanks to the scientists. And the clue to those early mistakes was the failure to recognize that what you get out of your scientific observations depends a great deal on how you look at them. If you ask a question in purely scientific terms, those are the only terms in which it can be answered. But how you interpret that answer will depend on something else—outside science. Do you remember that gorgeous hymn of Joseph Addison's:

> The spacious firmament on high,
> With all the blue ethereal sky,
> And spangled heavens, a shining frame,
> Their great original proclaim.
>
> The unwearied sun, from day to day,
> Doth his Creator's power display;
> And publishes to every land
> The work of an Almighty hand.

That may be right for Joseph Addison. But what about some of the other points of view? Pascal said how the vast silence of the stars frightened him: Gilbert Murray writes of the Graeco-Roman world, that 'their religion was overwhelmingly absorbed in plans of escape from the prison of the stars'. As another historian (Edwyn Bevan) puts it: 'When men looked up at the stars, they shuddered to see there the powers whose mysterious influence held them in a mechanism of iron necessity.'

I think we should be careful before we maintain that all men should be able to see God in the world of astrophysics. They may see the world of astrophysics; but they will not necessarily see God.

I said that it was the scientists who had encouraged us

to notice that the conclusions which we draw from an experiment depend considerably on the way we approach the whole matter. Let me say what I mean by this, and then illustrate it in terms of the problem of mind and brain.

Ever since J. J. Thomson, the former master of my own College at Cambridge, showed at the turn of the century that one of the most fundamental constituents of all matter was the electron, a very very tiny particle of electricity, people have tried to find out more about electrons—to know them better, to understand them, to picture them better, if you like. But for years they kept on running up against a snag. Sometimes the electron seemed to behave like a particle, a tiny billiard-ball, which you could imagine being at a particular place, or hitting some other particle and bouncing off. But at other times it was like a wave, or set of waves. You cannot then say that the electron is at any one particular place, it may be anywhere where the waves are: and furthermore (as you can observe if you watch the waves in the wake of a moving boat), one wave can pass right through another wave without being destroyed, or altered, and without bouncing off. So an electron was a wave, *or* a particle. Which was it? The answer is just this: both descriptions are correct, but you can only give one at a time: and the answer you get in any experiment depends on the way you set up the apparatus, that is, the way in which you asked the question. But clearly your real understanding of the nature of the electron is not complete until you have recognized both characteristics.

What I have just described for electrons is true of all matter; and it has now been absorbed into the whole framework of modern physics. The issue is important because the classification came from within science itself. For example, we are not comparing a scientist's view of something with an artist's; nor a physicist's with a chemist's or electrical engineer's. Even within the one discipline of physics there does not seem to be any one single view, independent of the observer. What the observer plans, or prepares for, determines in part what he gets from his experiment.

Now let us apply this principle to the scientific work of the anatomist, interested in the nature of the brain, and its possible relationship with mind and spirit. In the first place we shall not need any more to argue about a possible conflict of mind versus matter, as if we had to believe in just one or the other. There may perfectly well be two (or more) distinct ways of looking at mind. If that is the case, as I believe it to be, it is hopeless to expect that questions about the brain posed and answered in scientific terms can provide us with anything like a complete description of the mind. In the second place it is no earthly good attempting to get round the conflict which does not exist by trying to prove that 'mind is matter interpreted by the quantum theory' (or any other theory of physics or chemistry). For mind and matter are two different ways of looking at the same entity. If we ask a scientific question about the mind, our answer will be bound to be in terms of millions of nerve fibres and electric currents; if we ask other questions about it, we shall expect an answer in terms of beauty and aware-ness and pattern; and yet other questions, those which we may label as specifically religious (though I hate the phraseology as you will see later) will receive religious answers. The one answer is both a wave and a particle.

It is only when our answers get mixed up that we find trouble. Man is matter or mind, depending on how you look at him. But only the wise men of Gotham would mix the two together, and try to weigh his soul.

All this means that our experiments alone do not tell us anything about God. A little later I shall point out how it is the way that we look at our answers (even the scientific answers) that does tell us, and not the answers themselves. This will help us to see why every professional scientist is not automatically a Christian (though as a matter of fact the proportion is a lot higher than most folk suppose); for the scientist, by himself, just because of his specialization and the single type of question that he is obliged to ask, can never give a complete description of God; indeed he only sees his discoveries as revealing the work of God when he is prepared for something of that kind.

Thus the partial picture obtained by a scientist acquires religious significance only when looked at in the right way. This is important, for it should warn us against hoping to convert scientists to Christianity simply by discussing scientific matters. I want a name for this attitude of mind, without which scientific discoveries cannot be fully appreciated. If possible, the name should indicate the frame of mind which the scientist must bring to the interpretation of his work. As we have seen, it is not necessary that he should do so: but it is inescapably true that unless he does, he will not completely understand the significance of his work. May I call it the 'theistic attitude'? It is a horrid term, but I cannot think of a better. Professor J. P. Hodges once spoke of an 'Abrahamic presupposition'. That seems to me to go just a little farther than I need to go at the moment; and it is, if anything, even less easily intelligible. So let the 'theistic attitude' remain.

What does it mean? It may help us to clarify our mind if we compare two scientists, one with, the other without, this attitude. But of course both are scientists. Let us suppose, then, that we have a scientist without the theistic attitude. How will he interpret his work? To make the matter precise, what, for example, would he say of the nature of man? There would be lots of answers, according to the type of scientist that he was; but, if I may be allowed a little exaggeration, many of them would be more or less like this:

To the physicist, man is a machine (did not Descartes say: 'Give me matter and motion, and I'll construct the Universe'?); to the chemist man is an intricate series of nicely balanced biochemical reactions, of such a kind that a certain oracular Professor Tyndall, when presiding over the British Association some years ago, could confidently tell his audience that 'as the bile is a secretion of the liver, so the mind is a secretion of the brain'. But this is not all: to the psychologist man is a bundle of responses to varying stimuli; to the geneticist he is described in terms of heredity; to the anatomist his brain is no more than that conglomeration of nerve fibres and resonating electrical circuits that I have already described.

The tragedy lies just here; man *is* all these, but he is more than this. Conversely, the God who made him *is* all these. God *is* a great mathematician, God *is* a great artist, a great poet. But he is more. And we shall only begin to see all this if we accept what I called the 'theistic attitude'. If we do not, then the work of the scientist will not appear to say anything at all about God. There will be no revelation for us there; and our worship will be so much the more impoverished.

But suppose that we do accept the theistic attitude? What does it involve? Does it mean that we abandon scientific truth, in favour of something other-worldly, or spooky, or emotional? Not at all; scientific truth holds firm, and is the very platform on which we stand to get our wider view. What it does mean is that starting with the discoveries of science, and accepting in our minds the possibility that the world in which we live carries meaning, and can be interpreted in terms of a God, we allow our minds to dwell on it, to rest on it, to 'feel' it, to fit it in with what we know by other routes of the nature of this God. It is perfectly proper—as science itself has shown us—to approach the matter in other ways than one; the different views do not invalidate one another. In this case we shall find that the Universe does speak to us, and speaks to us through the scientists who, often enough, are God's unknowing mouthpiece.

Now let us suppose that, having accepted this theistic attitude, we are ready to hear what the Universe says to us. What do we learn from the exploring of the scientist?

Three things first—to some extent elementary, though to understand them in any full sense is to enter a new dimension of worship. I will call them power, time and fitness. Let us take them in turn.

Power. When the astronomer tells us of the number of the stars, and of the prodigious processes of atomic transformation that go on within them, refuelling their giant fires, our reaction may be one of terror, or it may be completely neutral, or it may be one of assurance. In very simplified terms, these are the reactions of the non-Christian (who is afraid), the pure scientist (who brings no other approach than the strictly scientific) and the Christian. And for us, who are Christian, how much richer our awareness becomes! For we hold a doctrine of creation; and believe that creation, whatever it was, was an act of God. The doctrine itself is an attempt to express our conviction that the very galaxies are the product of his power and his wisdom. And what power! The enormous space and the unthinkable energy are his space, his energy. But there is more yet. For some of the astrophysicists are coming to the view that creation was not a once-for-all process, some ninety thousand million years or more ago; but is still continuing; people like Hoyle, Gold, Bondi and Lyttleton at Cambridge, as well as others in other countries, have recently been giving cogent reasons for believing that new matter is continually being created, everywhere throughout the Universe; slowly but continuously. To the scientist, *qua* scientist, this may be nothing more than one new term in an equation, a new symbol that he must learn to manipulate in his algebra, as indeed it is in a recent scientific paper; but to us, if it is true (which is a scientific matter and not a religious one) it is one more sign of the continuing energy of God. It does not matter to us whether the theory of continuous creation is true or not; we shall know that in the course of time, perhaps a year or two. In either case what does matter is that our whole horizon of thought has been enlarged by the discoveries of physical science; God's limitless energy and power are revealed to those who explore and then reflect.

St. Augustine says in one part of his Confessions: 'Lord, when I consider my own life, it seems thou hast led me so carefully, so tenderly, thou canst have attended to no-one else. But when I see how thou hast led the whole world, and art still leading it, I am amazed thou hast had time for such as I.' St. Augustine knew nothing of the splendours of the heavens, such as we know. How much more poignant does his wonder become!

It is true with my second element, time. The world is not a mere 6,000 years old; but just as our scale of space and distance has had to be revolutionized, so has our time-scale. Millions of years, thousands of millions of years: this is the time scale in which we must think of God. Do you remember that phrase from our Bible: 'The Ancient of Days'; or that moment when God told Moses what he was to tell the people of Israel: 'I am that I am'? Does it not now take on a more luminous aspect than ever before? Is it not indeed unthinkably grander, finer, more compelling of our worship? Then let us thank God for the astrophysicists, his messengers.

Thirdly, what I called fitness. In recent years we have learnt how much more intricate is the physical world and its behaviour than ever we had thought before. That example of vitamin K, or of the cancer-producing chemicals, shows what I mean. It is as though everything had a peculiar fitness, a particular role to play in one great scheme—a purpose which could not be fulfilled other than by this highly-specialized component. Now as Christians we hold that this world and its inhabitants and all that is in it does form part of a divine scheme, in which, sometimes unknown or unseen by us, all things work together for good. When I think, as sometimes I do, on the peculiar way in which things seem to fit together in a great pattern, I feel a bit like Thomas Hardy in *The Dynasts*: you may perhaps remember how the Spirit of the Years takes the reader up to the top of a great mountain in Europe, and opens out to him a vision of the whole of the continent, seething with life; and he suddenly sees it as one whole, with the Alps as a backbone, and with mighty rivers as its arteries; and the thousands of its inhabitants as co-operators in a single enterprise. That vision is now magnificently enlarged, and become more detailed. The Psalmist could say:

> O Lord, how manifold are thy works!
> In wisdom hast thou made them all.

We shall want to say: thank God for those who sought out these details of chemistry and bio-chemistry and showed us the scale on which we must think of God's wisdom. For the explorers of this world are his messengers.

But we must be careful. For there is one trap into which it is very easy to fall; and to which we all succumb at some time or other. I am thinking of the danger of sentimentalizing about Nature. As I was preparing this essay, I was sitting in my study, and watching the birds on the lawn outside my window. There were two sparrows, engaged in love-play on the garden hose. How idyllic! How indicative of God's nature, we may be tempted to say; and many do say. But wait a moment; our picture of God cannot be painted so easily; the paleness of water-colours is not strong enough for God's delineation. There are some other birds by the side of those two sparrows; and these others are busily engaged in eating up thousands and thousands of little flying ants which have just hatched out of their eggs and are learning to move along the blades of grass. The great French insect-man Fabre has put on record the ghoulish story of the predatory wasps, and the fiendish nuptial rites of the Praying Mantis; and this should remind us that our

picture of God has got to resemble more the violence of
a sunset painting by Turner than, as one of my friends
once put it, a watery wash by a maiden aunt! Nature is
red in tooth and claw; and if in the end we come to
accept Fabre's own verdict on his studies, that all Nature
is 'obedient to a sublime law of sacrifice', we shall
mostly have to come to it in travail of soul; to assume
the theistic attitude will lead us into the deeps, if we
manage to avoid being merely sentimental, or superficial, or trivial. The scientists may be God's ministers
but he has made them messengers of flaming fire.

This is leading me to the heart of what I want to say.
When we look at the world through the eyes which the
scientist has lent to us, we shall not find easy solutions
to our difficulties, or a kind of sea-front holiday photo-
graph of God. And the reason is quite deep; it springs
out of the way in which we shall interpret the universe
that we see. Let me illustrate what I mean. A hundred
or so years ago, when scientific discoveries were beginning to flood in, some people used to liken God to a
watchmaker; they said that the world was most intri-
cately made, like a watch, and its very detailed con-
cordant character presupposed a watchmaker; no engine
without an engineer to design it; no watch without a
watchmaker; no world without a great designer, God.
This may be true, in some senses, but it is extremely
dangerous. For the watchmaker is outside the watch,
the engineer is independent of his engine; and he only
comes to it to set it going, or to interfere to repair it when
it goes wrong. Is that the kind of God that we shall infer
from science? God is not just the great First Cause,
separate from and other than his creation; if so, he's no
use to you and me; and he is not the God of Jesus Christ.

F

I would put it this way. The created world must not show us only what God is like; it must show us God.

This it can never do, without first the theistic attitude; and even then only as we bring to our interpretation something more specifically Christian. For the world that we touch and handle is not just the world that God made; it *is* God himself, his essence, his being. I remember the first time that I looked down a microscope and saw a bit of bone tissue being kept alive in a test-tube, and growing bit by bit as the various cells divided, and built up stage by stage their part of the living tissue; what would have been the knee bone of an embryo chicken. It was, for me then, a strange and rather awe-inspiring sight. I remember what I said to myself; it was not—'this is what God is like, always and everywhere building body and flesh and bone' (though of course that is quite correct); what I did say was this: 'Here *is* God in his very own self'; and so, as of a sudden, the glory; for here is God performing his daily task, and sustaining his creation. This is holy ground, it is none other than the House of God; no, more than that, it is his very self. We don't see what God is like, we actually see God.

This is why, in one sense, we are priests (do not mis-understand me, as I say this). Many of us who are scientists know this emotion from our own experience. To touch and handle even the so-called material things of this earth is to experience something of a sacrament. And so everything is different for us. There are some words of George Macleod's that I would quote here. He is thinking a bit along these lines:

When we realize that all our scientific discoveries are sacra-mental unveilings of the Body of our Lord; when we realize that we cannot lift a stone to build a fortification but the presence of God moves in to occupy the hole that we have made; when we grasp that the houses men live in (and not just the men who live in them) are offerings for his glory; and that the food men eat (and not just they who eat the food) are aspects of his presence; when the angels reveal (as science, that modern trumpet of the angels, does reveal) that the 'fulness of the whole earth is his glory', then we begin to know what it means that 'The Word became Flesh'.

Of course we need to bring our Christian experience to it; and we need to bring our theological insight into the fact of Christ; these are necessary to avoid becoming what would otherwise be pantheist, or animist. God *is* in the stone, the tree and the clod; but he is also in the very soul of man, he is 'maker, defender, redeemer and friend'.

And how much more glorious, more vigorous, more awe-ful our approach to God now becomes! There is a poem by Angela Morgan:

> I am aware
> As I go commonly sweeping a stair
> . . . .
> I am aware of a splendour that ties
> All the things of the earth to the things of the skies:
> Here in my body the heavenly heat,
> Here in my flesh the melodious beat
> Of the planets that circle Divinity's feet.

And not only 'my' body and 'my' flesh, but in all the created world. God is in it, we see him there; not a likeness of him, or a picture of him, but himself. Evolution, traced for us by the scientist, is seen by us as the travail of God's energy, creating man in his own image. No wonder it is shot through with pain and sacrifice and blood, like the travail of a woman with child. All things are part of a great design; but it is a living, growing and developing pattern, since God is in it. Here, and only here, is the beginning of our understanding of that 'sublime law of sacrifice' which Fabre saw throughout the animal world; and, no less, of that 'groaning' of the whole physical creation which St. Paul has described for us in his letter to the Romans. Creation is not what God did, or even what God does; but what he is. It is the finger of God that we see throughout the cosmos, and not the work of those fingers, when we receive the revelation of science.

There is a description given of Michael Faraday, the chemist; and it says that when he went to his prayers he forgot his science; and when he went into his laboratory, he closed the door on his religion. That is absolutely fatal, if what I have been saying is true. For the laboratory is the place of revelation, and the exploration itself is properly called a religious activity.

It may sound strange that I should claim all scientific study and research as being in essence religious. But I do. For the world is given: we receive it; and study it; we investigate it; we accept the position of creatureliness with respect to it. Any inquiry, which accepts the fact of creation (in whatever form, whether Hoyle's continuous creation or the older once-for-all type), and then relates its own activity to that fact, is an act of worship. It is the person who denies this who is narrow-minded: not, as is often thought, the Christian. Sir Lawrence Bragg, Lord Rutherford's successor at Cambridge, puts this very finely:

> When one has sought long for the clue to a secret of Nature, and is rewarded by grasping some part of the answer, it comes as a blinding flash of revelation; it comes as something new, more

simple and at the same time more subtle, and more aesthetically satisfying, than anything one could have created in one's own mind. This conviction, [he says,] is of something revealed, and not something imagined.

When you think of it like this, it is not hard to see why Science plays its part in the understanding of God, and shares his revelation. That is why so many of the great men of Science, from Newton and Galileo through to Max Planck and Sir Arthur Eddington, have felt, as they studied, that they were indeed tracing the finger of God throughout the cosmos; they were developing a language in which God and God's work could be described. But of course there are plenty of languages, and few of us would claim that all the treasure of literature could be confined within any one of them.

If I try to summarize what I have been trying to say, it might go like this.

Scientific study, by itself, will never lead us to God. But if there goes with it what I called the theistic attitude, which for us means a belief in the God of Jesus Christ, then it can speak to us, and reveal the splendour of God. And yet not just the splendour of God, but God himself. It becomes a revelation of him, leading us into the deep waters, but gloriously enriching our awareness and our worship.

Yet even now we must be careful, so my last word is a word of warning. Science cannot base our faith; it can illuminate it. We must not claim too much for man's discovery, however splendid. If you go into an architect's office, you can see the drawings for a new building. You may look at an elevation: you get something out of it, some notion of what the building looks like from outside: it is a revelation of the nature of the building. But it is not complete. Or you may look at a plan. It will show you the floor space: but it is not complete either. Nor are the sections by themselves, however interesting and suggestive. You need them all, if you would really know the building; and of course there is only one building, of which these all are partial views, supplementing one another.

It is a bit like that when we think of our knowledge of God. Science, art, theology, poetry—these are like the plans and the elevations of the building, supplementing each other's incompleteness, and building up together a whole and living reality. Someone said at the end of a recent book—a scientific book, as a matter of fact—'there are no fragmentary answers'. Our science—man's exploring of the nature of God—will be seen in its proper perspective only from beyond science; our religion, too, will become fully alive for us only when the splendour of the world revealed by science is bodied forth in awe, and in worship and understanding.

PART II

GOD AND MAN

The Idea of Revelation in Religion

NORMAN SNAITH

THIS chapter is an essay on the ideas of inspiration and revelation in the Old Testament. For Jew and Christian, this is the proper place to begin. It develops into a study of Certainty, since this is the real crux of the problem.

The earliest theories of revelation and inspiration in the Old Testament depend on the assumption that every event is caused by a personal agent. If, then, any particular event is obviously not caused by a human personal agent, it must have been caused by a non-human personal agent. The technique of revelation therefore consisted in the selection of, or the staging of, events which might fairly be presumed to be caused by the God of Israel. Such an event would be one which took place in a shrine dedicated to the God of Israel, or it could involve the manipulation of some instrument sacred to him, and manipulated by a person sacred to him.

This, for instance, was the theory of the sacred lot, which in pre-exilic times was divination by Urim and Thummim. This was done by means of an ephod. This ephod was not the linen ephod worn by the priests, which was a pair of very short linen drawers, nor was it the elaborate arrangement fastened to the High Priest's robe in post-exilic times. Possibly it was an image, small enough for a man to be able to carry it when he was running for his life (compare 1 Samuel 22:20 with 21:9 and 23:9), and portable enough to be 'brought hither' by Abiathar, David's priest and companion in his freebooting days. There was, we presume, a hollow in this ephod, and in the hollow two objects. What exactly these objects were, we have no means of knowing. We do know, however, that the question which was asked of this oracle had to be framed so as to be capable of the answer 'yes' and 'no', and there could be 'no answer'. The most likely suggestion is that they were two flat discs, white (say) on one side and (say) black on the other. If the two whites came up, the answer was Thummim (i.e. 'Perfect'), and so was 'Yes'; if the two blacks came up, the answer was Urim (i.e. 'Curses'); if the discs came up, one white and one black, then there was no answer. Presumably this is what happened persistently when Saul, bereft of divine counsel after the death of Samuel, received no answer by dreams, by prophets or by Urim (1 Samuel 28:6).

This verse in 1 Samuel refers to other ways in which it was believed the will of God could be revealed. The theory of divination by dreams is that in them there are thoughts and visions over which the recipient has no control. If he is a sacred person, or if he is a devout seeker sleeping in a holy place (Incubation), then presumably the dreams are created and controlled by the deity of the place. Compare the experience of the young Marius in Walter Pater's *Marius the Epicurean*: 'dreams, living ministers of the god, more likely to come to one in his actual dwelling-place than elsewhere.' Divine revelation in dreams is found also in the first two chapters of St. Matthew (1:20, 2:13, 19). The verse in 1 Samuel refers also to divine revelation through prophets. The reference here is to the type of ecstatic prophet who was a characteristic of Canaanite religion, much earlier than and nothing to do with the dancing dervish of very much later Islamic times. These prophets were either borderline cases of men who were easily subject to abnormal, uncontrolled behaviour, or men who deliberately induced themselves into a state of frenzy. In either case they ceased to be in control of their faculties. Cf. 1 Samuel 19:24. Sometimes this hypnotic state was induced by music, as in the case of Elisha (2 Kings 3:2). Here again we have the same theory as before; cries and sounds, movements of the limbs and so forth, were caused by a personal agent, who in these cases could not be the man himself.

There are other types of divination mentioned in the Old Testament, all depending upon an 'uncaused' event, and doubtless some of these types, if not all of them, were at one time practised by the Hebrews. Ezekiel 21:21 refers to two of them. One is the examination of the liver of a slaughtered animal; there is plenty of evidence that this science of hepatoscopy was practised in Palestine in ancient times. The other is divination by the casting of arrows, the direction in which the arrows point, when haphazardly thrown, to the accompaniment of the proper words, being the determining factor. The idea that 'uncaused' events are nevertheless caused in the last resort by God is not confined to the practice of divination alone. The Syrian archer 'drew his bow at a venture', and the arrow mortally wounded Ahab of

Israel. The writer (1 Kings 22:34) infers that the arrow shot at random into the air against the Israelite armies was nevertheless guided by God.

All these types of divination were practised by the Hebrews in common with other peoples. They are part of the heritage in common with other races in general; in particular they form part of the general corpus of magic-religious practice which is the apparatus of 'natural religion', that religion which has grown up with man, and can be traced by evolutionist historians; it forms a general corpus of practice and custom on which all religions draw, whatever type that religion may be. We turn therefore to the differences in ideas of revelation and divination, because it is in the difference between one cult and another, between one religion and another, between one people and another, that we can find the genius, the significance, the distinctive element in that cult, religion, or people.

It is impossible to say when and where the changes began amongst the Hebrews. Most writers of the last fifty years have accepted the uncritical assumptions of so many scientific writers that everything everywhere depends on evolutionary development. For instance, it has been assumed without question that Tylor, Frazer and company are right in that monotheism arrived late as an evolutionary development from animatism, animism, fetichism, ancestor worship, polytheism, henotheism, and so forth. Actually nobody ever got monotheism out of that kind of thing. Why is there no monotheism anywhere except among and arising from the Hebrew prophets? Environment and growth are not enough to explain Israel's religion, and they can be made to be enough only by misinterpreting the literature. It is customary to say that the new development, the distinctive development, began with the prophets, but, 'how did Israel become a nation with such faith in its God that its very existence was conceived to be a miracle of grace? The prophets did not invent this remarkable conception since it existed before them.'[1] Certainly as early as Moses at the Bush (Exodus 3) we get a Wholly Other, and embedded in the story is the fact of a compulsion, the driving forwards of a man who is unwilling and genuinely believes himself to be incapable. Here we have something other than the Natural Religion which Tylor, Frazer and even moderns like Julian Huxley discuss. They speak and write of a religion which is the outcome of man's speculation and philosophizing, a 'religion without revelation'. It is composed of all sorts of projections, personalizations, complexes and the like. It shows itself in magico-religious rites such as fill the pages of *The Golden Bough*, in turnings and postures, and processions, blood-lettings and sacrifices of every type, bird and beast and man. It shows itself in what Van Gennep called 'les rîtes de passages', the apotropaic ceremonies which cluster round all 'passage' times, when nature and man pass from one house of life to another—the change-over of the seasons, the mid-season period, nights of the new moon and the full moon, birth, puberty, marriage, death—all occasions which are still the basis of religious exercises in all religions which have any cult at all. But in the Old Testament, there is something else, something which does not spring from the earth and is not earthy. It is not the product of man's aspirations and strivings,

[1] G. Ernest Wright, *The Old Testament against its Environment*, p. 13.

his guesses and imaginations, his struggle to persuade himself that death is not the end. (In this last respect, incidentally, it is worth notice that the period when Monotheism is most clearly expressed, and the time of what we will call the progress of Monotheism, is the time when the Hebrews believed least in any life after death.) This something else is from outside man, and it is contrary to all man's schemes for self-realization. The theme is expressed at its clearest in the Old Testament in Isaiah 53. In as much as the nature of the bud is most clearly to be seen when the flower has fully opened, the full blossoming is to be seen in the Crucified Christ. This is the revelation which shines through till the bright light of noonday makes it clear. And the measure of its contrariness to the product of evolutionary revelation is the fact that to this day Christ Crucified is a stumbling-block to the Jews and is foolishness to the Greeks—the former being those who speak of religion primarily in terms of ethics, and the latter being those who believe that a Utopia can actually be established on this earth by the wisdom of the human spirit.

It is possible to see these 'Other' ideas breaking through the crust of natural religion. One example of this is to be seen in the story of Saul. Here we have an ethicizing process. All fits of uncontrolled behaviour which seized Saul between the time of his being anointed (1 Samuel 10:1) and the time of David's being anointed (1 Samuel 16:13) are ascribed to the *ruach-adona* (the Spirit of the LORD), but after 16:13 the writer carefully avoids the use of this specially sacred term. He says that the *ruach-adonai* departed from Saul, 'and an evil *ruach* from the LORD troubled him'. It was still a 'spirit' (*ruach*) that troubled Saul, and it still had to be a *ruach* from the LORD, but it was not *the* Spirit of the LORD which inspires the LORD's king. And later, the writer uses the phrase *ruach-elohim*, the word *elohim* being the general Semitic word for 'god'. Here the Sacred Name is avoided altogether.

The writer evidently finds himself in a difficulty. He cannot deny that Saul is still subject to fits of uncontrolled behaviour, but it is equally clear to him that the general theory that all such behaviour is due to the spirit of the LORD is faulty. Another solution is attempted in 1 Kings 22:1–28. The four hundred court prophets urge Ahab to attack the Syrians in Ramoth Gilead and promise him victory. They were wrong, but right or wrong, sincere or sycophant, no one was prepared to deny that they were inspired. They exhibited all the signs of it; compare the State Oracle described in Heinrich Harrer, *Seven Years in Tibet*. It was still held that all such manifestations and the words then spoken were due to Jehovah, God of Israel. The explanation of Micaiah was that Jehovah had deliberately sent a lying spirit in order to entice Ahab to his doom. This explanation is paralleled by Jeremiah's woeful cry: 'O Lord, thou hast deceived me, and I was deceived' (20:7), when he found that he had spoken what he believed to be God's Word, and had been wrong. The stage here reached is: there is an inspiration which can be ascribed definitely to the God of Israel, but there is also an inspiration which can be ascribed to him only 'with intent to deceive'. Clearly, if God is a God of truth and righteousness, the whole problem remains yet to be solved.

How then can inspiration be tested? Can it be tested by its results? There are two attempts to do this in

Deuteronomy. The first is Deuteronomy 13:1–5. It was customary for the prophet to produce some sign in order to authenticate his message, and it was believed that if the sign was indeed produced, the word of the prophet was true and it would certainly come to pass. The sign was regarded as the first step in the actual fulfilment of what God had already decided. When once God had thus begun to act, the rest was inevitable. King Ahaz did not want Isaiah to produce a sign (Isaiah 7:12), because he believed, in common with everyone else, that if once the sign was forthcoming, the rest was inevitable. He did not want to be involved to any degree in the policy which Isaiah advocated and which Isaiah said was the word of God. The only way to avoid the ful-filment of what Isaiah had to say was to avoid the sign. But Isaiah's reply was that Ahaz was going to have the sign whether he liked it or not.

The second attempt is in Deuteronomy 13:1–5. Even if a sign is given, there is no guarantee that the word is from God. Here is a new test. 'How shall we know the word which the Lord hath not spoken?' The answer is: it all depends on whether the word proves true. If the thing does not happen, then it is not the word of God: and this holds, sign or no sign. It is clear that the problem of inspiration is far from being solved. Even in the New Testament, the problem is still urgent. In 1 John 4:1 we are bidden not to believe every spirit. They have to be tested. That is, we are not necessarily to believe that a man is inspired of God, whatever he himself may say about it, or however sure he himself may be about it. Neither is the test of truth in itself enough. If the man is speaking of the future, his own mother wit may lead him to the truth. And the man may be as godly as

anybody can desire, and still be wrong. What is the test?
Or is there indeed any such thing as inspiration? If there
is such a thing, how can we distinguish between 'the
spirit of truth' and 'the spirit of error'?

The whole matter rests upon assumptions, and no man
can possibly prove either that there is such a thing as
inspiration by God or that there is not inspiration by
God. Certain thoughts come into a man's mind. In
some cases he may be able to trace them in his own previous thinking. In other cases they may come 'like a bolt
from the blue'. If he can trace the development in his
own previous thinking, does that necessarily mean that
it is all 'out of his own head'? The answer is 'No'. It
may be out of his own head in the sense that he has built
it all up himself, thought by thought in logical sequence.
On the other hand, it may be equally true that some
power other than himself has guided the process. He
cannot tell. He will most easily assume that he alone is
responsible for the development of his thoughts, and
this will be assumed by those who hold that religion is a
human projection. It will be most readily, indeed, assumed by them, because he is doing with his own thinking process what they say he is doing about the outside
world. But for him to assume that he himself is wholly
responsible for his own thought-processes is pure
assumption. How does he know where the thoughts came
from, whether solely from previous thoughts or from
some outer prompting? All he knows is that he has had
such thoughts. How they came, or whence, is nothing
but assumption. Or, on the other hand, he has a thought
'out of the blue'. He may call it 'a sudden inspiration'.
How does he know that it is 'out of the blue'? It may be
equally as in the previous case, a product of his own

processes of thought, but with the stages not clear to
him. All that may have happened is that he has jumped
one or two stages.

Everything, therefore, depends on the assumptions.
If we begin by asserting that all thoughts come from the
conscious or from the subconscious and so forth, then
there is no such thing as inspiration and revelation. If
we begin by allowing that thought can be influenced by
other minds, then we can assume the existence of such
things as telepathy, precognition, and the rest—any one
of them, or all of them. It may be that this is what
'inspiration' is: the impact of other human minds. We
can ascribe everything to, say, telepathy, which we cannot account for by the ordinary processes of thought.
Again, it all depends upon whether we allow the existence
of such a thing. But again, we can assume the existence
of a God who can influence the minds of men. No man is
in a position to deny this, for no man can prove that
there is no God. He can produce all sorts of explanations
for God-consciousness, but all his explanations depend
on his own assumptions, which may be adequate enough
for him, but are certainly not adequate for the God-
conscious man.

I find nowhere any certainty on these lines.

My solution is as follows—actually it goes back to
Jeremiah. His first attempt at prophecy as a young man
is to be found in Jeremiah 1:13 ff. He saw a bubbling
cauldron, and it meant trouble was boiling up for Judah.
It meant 'trouble from the north'. Perhaps there was
something in the set of the pot that suggested it; more
likely 'trouble from the north' was the regular phrase
of these prophets of disaster, since that was invariably
the direction from which trouble came. More specific-

ally, the reference seems to be to the Scythian invasion of the early years of King Josiah. Jeremiah expected them to conquer Jerusalem, to set up their thrones in the place of judgement ('the entering of the gates') and there deliver sentence on prisoners and captured city. But he was wrong; Jerusalem was not taken by the Scythians. Jeremiah's second attempt at prophecy involved his support of the Deuteronomic reforms (Jeremiah 11), but once more he was wrong, because the Jerusalem priests were anxious only for their own aggrandisement, and any reforms that were introduced were merely superficial. He had spoken twice, each time sincerely believing that he was inspired by God and that his words were a divine revelation; each time he was wrong. So he remained silent, and determined to speak no more in God's Name (20:9). But there came a time when he could no longer be silent; it was like 'a burning fire shut up in his bones' and he could no longer hold it in. So once more he spoke as a prophet, and continued; but this time he was right, and it was indeed the word of the Lord which he spoke.

Jeremiah's career was curiously at variance with his character; it is all the time as though he was driven on, pushed, thrust forward—true to his name, which probably means 'Jah throws, shoots'. (It may mean 'Jah looseneth' i.e. from the womb.) Some men are never afraid to stand alone, and in fact enjoy it. When Athanasius was told that all the world was against him, he was not in the least distressed, and probably rather enjoyed the experience. But Jeremiah was different. As soon as a check came, he tended to doubt and question himself. He himself was not naturally the man to stand alone. Again, if ever there was a man who was born to be

G

husband and father, it was this man Jeremiah. Yet he found himself constrained to be wifeless and childless because of a conviction which came to him that this was God's will for him (16:1). Yet again, few men can have loved their country more fervently than he, but his message was 'Surrender'; it was borne in upon him that to struggle for freedom and independence was vain and would bring disaster—far better surrender to the Babylonians and accept what terms they must.

Now, here we have a man naturally friendly, made for companionship, with an innate dislike of being and standing alone, but at the same time cut off and isolated from all, even from his own family, who tried to murder him. And in that long silence after his first two failures, he was driven into a companionship with God such as no man knew before his time. The result was that next time he said 'Thus saith the Lord', it was indeed the saying of the Lord. Presumably, when a prophet says 'Thus saith the Lord', he means that deep down in his heart, right at the centre of his convictions, he believes that what he says is true. He believes also that this word has come to him from outside himself, a conviction that has been forced upon him. After Jeremiah's enforced silence, God was in his heart, and Jeremiah was thoroughly and completely convinced of this.

'Religion at root is a matter of personal relationship with God.' Such a statement assumes that there is a God, and it assumes also that it is possible for God and a man to be aware of each other. Is there any possible proof of this? The answer is that there are two types of proof, each proper to its own sphere. There is the type that is used in formal logic, and this is what is usually called 'proof'. I doubt whether even this can 'prove' anything

THE IDEA OF REVELATION IN RELIGION   83

at all; all that can be done is to show that the conclusion is not contradictory to the assumptions. The other type of proof is that which belongs to the world of personal relationships. Here there is a certainty at least as sure as that which can be found through formal logic. This certainty is to be found in the confidence and trust which exist between husband and wife, between true and firm friends of the David–Jonathan, Roland–Oliver type. It is hard to say in what this mutual confidence and certainty consists, for it is not because of this or that. It is a case of 'the soul of Jonathan was knit with the soul of David and Jonathan loved him as his own soul' (1 Samuel 18:1), where 'soul' (Hebrew *nephesh*) means 'life, person, individuality, inner being. . .'. This is the type of certainty which belongs to religion, which at root is a matter of personal relationship. For my part (since here there must be personal witness) this is the kind of certainty I have about God, and I think it was the type of certainty which Jeremiah had about God. It is not based, for me, on any so-called mystical experience, and I am not aware of any psychological state which could even border on hallucination. I think the same is true of Jeremiah. Paul was another man who was very, very sure about this matter, but he had a strange trancelike experience outside Damascus, and wrote later to the Corinthian church in strange, abnormal terms (2 Corinthians 12:1–10). He may therefore have been abnormal to the extent that he could easily be deluded into imagining that a psychological condition was more than subjective. But there is no evidence that Jeremiah was of this type. He was simply and plainly sure about God, precisely in the same way that he would have been sure about wife or children. I would say for myself that nobody ever argued me into this certainty about God, and I am quite sure that nobody can ever argue me out of it. It does not depend upon that type of argument. It depends upon that inner conviction which belongs to the realm of personal relationships. And in ordinary human experience, it is this kind of thing that ultimately counts most. This is why a man will do what common sense calls a stupid thing for his friend, why husband and wife will sacrifice everything for each other, parents for children—and all the time, other people will see plainly that their conduct is beyond reason. For instance, consider the way in which a wife will cling to a husband who is good-for-nothing. Everybody knows he is good-for-nothing; she knows herself he is so. But she will still cling to him and stand by him. Or consider the way in which a parent will stick by a boy who is no good. It may be said that there is pride of possession at the root, but it is a queer sort of selfish possession which leads folks to do such strange things. Indeed, if psychologists can speak of such loyalty and self-sacrifice as being self-realization or some such thing, then words can mean anything and not even the psychologists themselves can have any confidence in any thought or suggestion of their own.

I hold therefore that when we speak of inspiration and revelation, we are speaking of such certainty as this. The prophet speaks of that concerning which he is certain in his own heart, and to whatever extent he is sure about God in this personal way, to that extent the prophet is right. He must speak what he believes to be the will of God. It is possible that he may still be deluded. As to that we all have to wait till the Judgement Day when the secrets of all hearts shall be revealed. Apart from this certainty, I can find no chance of any at all. History proves nothing, for there never can be any history written or spoken about except according to some theory of the speaker or writer. Even if he tried to write down only what has happened, he still has a theory of history. Either there is a chain of cause and effect or else it is just 'One damned thing after another': either way, it is the speaker's assumption, and he has no means of proving the one any more surely than the other. If the proof is the evidence of the centuries, none of us will be here to see it. If there is nothing apart from this phenomenal world, what does it matter anyway? Is it not as sensible for the earth to be disintegrated by some atomic bomb as for it ultimately to become a dead world? Or equally to keep on keeping on? There is as much reason in one as in another.

Therefore I would say that the certainty which the Christian has is the only approach to certainty anyone can ever have. Apart from this, he must learn to stand on his own feet, and Ajax-like defy his own lightning— if he can.

The Christian View of Man

DAVID CAIRNS

THE German philosopher Schopenhauer was one day sitting hunched up on a seat in the Berlin Zoo, sunk in profound reflection. One of the attendants saw him, and not unnaturally put him down as a sinister-looking character. So he went up to him, and asked peremptorily, 'Who are you?' Schopenhauer shook off his abstraction, pondered the question for a moment or two with immense seriousness, and then broke out vehemently, 'I wish to God I knew.'

Schopenhauer's problem has not been settled finally yet. Indeed man has been defined as 'the being who is always in search of himself'. But while a complete answer is not to be expected, yet there is a great deal that has been learnt, and much that we are learning today about human nature. And since man is a complex being, there are many different kinds of experts who have something important to say about him. For example, chemistry can tell us something, the biologists can tell us more. The doctors have made a very important contribution to our knowledge here, and so have the psychologists. Indeed the psychologists have convinced us that there is a large area of our personality, which is not only hidden from our direct view, but actually unconsciously concealed from us by ourselves. Then there is light thrown on human nature by the great historians. No one could read carefully the story of the Syracusan Expedition by

Thucydides without knowing that his knowledge of man and destiny had been enriched. And then there are the great poets and novelists. When you close Tolstoy's *War and Peace*, you know something more about the 'grandeur and misery' of man than you did before you opened it for the first time.

Then there are the philosophers; they can tell us much about human nature—and indeed at the moment they are very busy doing so, opening up new fields of knowledge to us. And we must not forget in this list the contribution that some of us would count the most important of all, the contribution made by the Bible and the Christian Faith, as it has been expounded by the great theologians.

It would be a big mistake to assume that any one of these sources of knowledge about man was the only one to be trusted. This would be the case for example, if a Christian theologian were to deny that biology had anything to teach us about man and his history, or a chemist should claim that only the experimental sciences had something worth-while to tell us about him. It was, I think, the 'Radio Padre' who during the war pointed out that (as prices then stood) the market value of the chemical constituents of the human body (mostly water!) was just about 4s. 8½d. But no one in his senses would think of assessing the value of a human being at that price!

But since truth is in the last resort one, and without contradictions, we must believe that in the end there will be a harmony between the various things that the various experts tell us about man. Of course we must be ready to admit that in the course of thought some things will be shown up as errors, and it is clear that contradictions

have arisen and do arise. I wish to put forward the suggestion that in dealing with this subject, man, disagreements between two experts usually occur because one
expert has invaded the territory which really belongs to
another, and thus has come to conclusions which he has
no right to hold. I am thinking especially here of the
disagreements which have arisen between Christian
theologians on the one hand and scientists on the other.
Here the fault has sometimes been on the side of the
theologians, and sometimes on the side of the scientists.
For example, I believe that the famous conflict in 1860
between Samuel Wilberforce and T. H. Huxley, at the
Meeting in Oxford of the British Association, was an
occasion when the theologian Wilberforce was wrong,
opposing Huxley's account of the origins of the human
race on the grounds that the first chapters of Genesis
gave a different account. On the other hand when a
scientist passes from saying that there is very good
evidence that the human race is descended from a mammalian ancestry, and not created all at once from dust,
and goes on to claim that man is therefore nothing more
than the product of variation, environment and the
struggle for life, then he has passed from the field of
science, where he has a real authority, to the realm of
philosophy, and is making a philosophical statement—
incidentally the expression of a very bad philosophy.
He is, of course at liberty to make philosophical statements, about man or anything else, but let him be
clear about one thing, that in so doing he cannot claim
the prestige which he may rightly be accorded in his
own sphere, where every step has to be tested by such
practical experiments as are fitting in that particular
science.

There are indeed conflicts between the teaching of Christian theologians and certain philosophers. And these are on rather a different footing from the conflicts to which I have been referring between scientists and theologians. Here too, since truth is one, there must be some process of testing and verifying the claims of different statements to truth; and what this verification can be, is at this moment one of the open questions on the borderland of philosophy and theology.

There is a point which must here be made about Christian faith as a source of knowledge about man. Christian faith claims to rest upon revelation; we believe that God has told us something about himself which we could never have found out by ourselves. But when we say this, we are in danger of being misunderstood. The words suggest that what has been revealed are certain propositions about God. And strictly speaking this is not true. What has happened is that God has revealed, disclosed himself to us. I can take an illustration from human friendship. When a stranger introduces himself to me, and we become friends, he reveals himself to me. This friendship may mean a very great deal for my life, and it is a thoroughly personal relation. But it has one inevitable result. My knowledge of him can be put down in black and white, and this knowledge can be passed on to another person who does not know my friend. And so in the case of God; his revelation is always a personal thing, but it has resulted in what Christian theologians call the Doctrine of God, and this doctrine can be examined even by people who do not claim any personal acquaintance with God. The great source of this doctrine of God is the Bible, which is the record of God's personal revelation to men. The aim of the Bible is to introduce men to this personal relation, and not merely to add to their knowledge about God. But undoubtedly it claims to tell us true things about him. This is not revealed knowledge, strictly speaking, but knowledge which results from revelation. And of course its validity can be called in question by those who consider the claim to revelation, which the Bible makes, to be an illusion. It is, further, the Christian claim that in revealing himself to us, God has told us about ourselves, and also about his purposes with the world. For we hold that man is so inseparably linked up with God, that there are essential things about our nature that we cannot know until we know it in its relationship to God. There is therefore a Christian Doctrine of Man, as there is a Christian Doctrine of the World, and a Christian Doctrine of God. These Doctrines claim to be the result of revelation, and Christians claim that none of them is in conflict with the legitimate findings of any of the sciences, or of history.

Now what in fact does the Bible teach about man? Part of what it says is to be found in the first chapters of Genesis, and as we examine the two accounts given there of man's origins, it will seem at first that here is a flagrant contradiction of what science says; and that here it is not science which is to blame for transgressing its legitimate boundaries, but the Bible. But I must ask the reader to have patience.

The Bible's teaching about man's nature is part of a larger whole—the history of God's dealings with mankind, and while the Bible picture of man is everywhere implicit, yet it is summed up in one phrase that is repeated several times in the first chapters of Genesis—and then not again till the later pages of the New Testament. The Bible tells us that man was created in the image and likeness of God.

There are actually two creation stories in the first two chapters of Genesis.[1] The earlier and simpler one is to be found in Genesis 2 from the fourth verse onwards, and belongs probably to the eighth century B.C. In this account the phrase 'image of God' does not occur. The story is told here that God formed man out of the dust of the ground, and breathed into his nostrils the breath of life, so that man became a living soul. God placed the man in a pleasant garden of fruit trees, and set him to tend it. God brought before him the various beasts, for which the man chose names. Then follows the story of the creation of the woman, who was formed out of a rib of the man while he was in a deep sleep which God had induced. The woman was created in order that she might give to the man a true fellowship which none of the animals could supply. There follows the story of the first temptation and sin, followed by the expulsion of the human pair from the garden. In this story it is clear that a humble origin is assigned to man, and yet the breath of God is breathed into him to make him a living being. He is given a certain authority over the animals, and a certain dignity which they do not share, for none of them can give him the fellowship which the woman is created to give.

The other story of creation is to be found in Genesis 1. It was probably put into its final form in the fifth century B.C., and tells how each class of living things was created, after the Divine Word fashioned light and the habitable earth and stars. Plants, trees, fish, reptiles and mammals were called into being by the uttering of the Divine Word.

[1] See also Professor Hooke's chapter, pp. 36–40.

But before the creation of man there comes a pause, and counsel is taken in the heavenly places. Then God creates man and woman in his own image and likeness. In this account there is no story of the temptation and fall of man.

On the meaning of this phrase 'In the image and likeness of God' more ink has been spent—I will not say spilled—from the days of the early rabbinical scholars, than over almost any other. The early Christian Fathers had their interpretations, the Roman Church and the Reformers differed upon it, and still today it is a bone of theological contention and the subject of loss of temper.

But I think that it would be fair to say that in general the conclusion reached today is this, that when the Old Testament writer said 'image' he meant the same thing as he meant when he said 'likeness', and referred to a quality, I might say a dignity of man's being, which was in some way akin to God's being, or was planned with a view to a resemblance to God's being. Further, that this character was not lost through man's sin. That it remains seems to be conclusively proved by Genesis 9:5–6, where God says to Noah and his sons that he will require any man or beast that has killed a human being, to be put to death also, and that for this reason, that man was created in God's image.[1] The unspoken but undoubted implication is that man is sacred, by virtue of his very existence as man. It must further be noted that this sacredness remains, in a world where sin has

[1] There is nothing said here as to whether the penalty is exacted for murder only or for accidental killing. In Numbers 35 we read of cities of refuge whither men who had killed accidentally might flee for safety, with God's approval.

entered, for no-one will claim that Noah and his con-temporaries are pictured by Genesis as sinless. It is also clear that, in virtue of this dignity of his existence, man is given dominion by God over all the plants and animals in the world. Such is the teaching of the first chapters of Genesis about human nature.

Now it is but natural that at this point the objection will be raised that here clearly two accounts are given, of the creation of the world and man, which contain clear contradictions of the legitimate conclusions of natural science.

It is indeed remarkable how many things in the account in Genesis 1 chime in with the order of the actual creation of plants and animals, as science has disclosed it, but we must admit that the world is im-mensely older than the Bible writers thought, and that man was almost certainly descended from an ape-like ancestry. Further he was almost certainly not literally created from dust, and then the woman an hour or two later. True, these conclusions are not yet accepted by all Christian people, but they have been accepted by the large majority of those best fitted to judge—and that for the reason that science is within its rights when it makes its statements about man's ancestry and the time period that has elapsed since men appeared on the earth. Christian theologians have no right to dictate to scientists what conclusions they are to come to on scientific matters. It was just as wrong for Bishop Wilber-force to believe that the literal acceptance of the Genesis accounts was a necessary article of faith for Christians as it was for the persecutors of Galileo three hundred years earlier to force from him the following recantation 'I Galileo, being in my seventieth year, being a prisoner

and on my knees, and before your Eminences, having
before my eyes the Holy Gospel, which I touch with my
hands, abjure, curse and detest the error and the heresy
of the movement of the earth.'

What were the motives behind the demand that the
Creation Stories be taken as a literal transcript of
historic fact? There were, I think, two. First there was
an erroneous belief that if the Scriptures were inspired,
then the inspiration guaranteed the literal truth of every
detail recorded in them. And second there was the conviction that if man had not been created literally as
Genesis says, then man's special dignity and status were
lost. This was the fear that gave rise to Wilberforce's
gibe about Huxley being descended from an ape. But
this was clearly a mistaken fear. Just as the claim of
evolutionists would be mistaken if they asserted that
because man had a sub-human ancestry, therefore there
was in him nothing which was not in that sub-human
ancestry. Since there is in man clearly a wonderful
quality which is not in the animals, it is clear that we can
in a genuine sense believe that man's existence is a special
creation of God, even though he be descended from a
sub-human ancestry.

If, then, we cease to make the claim that the creation
stories in Genesis are literal transcripts of historic fact,
this does not mean that they have neither value nor
truth. They convey very deep truth, and that fact remains whether their writers and creators thought that
they were writing literal history, or not.

The Creation stories say first of all, at least this, that
nature and man owe their being to God. They are therefore not divine, but they are in essence good, and part
of God's original intention. Further the stories tell us

that there is a mysterious kinship between God and man. Man is indeed a part of nature, but he is also raised above nature. He is sacred, and must be treated as such. Further, the story of the Fall tells us that there is something wrong with the world, and particularly with man, and that for this flaw God is not directly responsible. The world as we know it, and man as we know him, are not what God meant them to be, but something is tragically wrong, and for this wrongness we share responsibility. Man is not just something which is not yet fully perfect, he is alienated from God. And then lastly the Creation story indicates that God is not content to leave it at that; he will bring things in order again. There will be a struggle with the powers of evil which in the end will result in their final defeat, and in a mysterious way man himself will be the agent of victory over evil and sin.[1]

Now in our discussion of the Old Testament teaching about man we must not confine ourselves to the first chapters of Genesis. I have only dealt with them at such length because of the difficulty they have caused to people who wished to believe, but thought that this involved a literal acceptance of these two accounts as historic fact.

It is, I think, fair to say that the picture given above agrees with the general picture of man given in the Old Testament. Man is created by God for communion with himself, and as such is sacred. This remains true, though in places a merciless policy against the enemies of Israel is urged in God's name. But if we look at the writings of the prophets, especially Amos, we find that there God's judgement is proclaimed, not only on Israel and Judah,

[1] See Genesis 3:15.

but also on the surrounding heathen races. And in each case the reason for this coming judgement is the harsh and unjust treatment of human beings. Two things can be inferred from this. First, for Amos, and the God for whom he speaks, man as such is sacred, and those who deal mercilessly with him, whether the injured man be Jew or heathen, will incur God's judgement. Secondly, not only should Israel and Judah, to whom God had specially revealed himself, know better than to be merciless, but so should the heathen; the heathen also are guilty of sinning against the light; that is, they too know, or could have known God. *There is no man to whom God does not speak*.

And this teaching fits within a wider framework in the Old Testament. All men, created in the image, are yet sinners, and cannot free themselves. But God in his mercy is preparing a world salvation, and will bless all peoples through a wider and nobler covenant than the first covenant which he made with the Hebrew people in old days.

In the Old Testament there is one psalm which is of special relevance to our theme, though in it the term 'image of God' is not mentioned in so many words. This is the eighth psalm, which is an eloquent and moving song of praise to God for his glory revealed in the heavens and moon and the stars, and then in his kindness to man. The psalmist goes on to ask 'What is man that thou art mindful of him?' But here, unlike some modern astronomers, he is not thinking with despair that man is too insignificant for the God of nature to take any care for him. The psalmist is quite sure of one thing, that God *has* shown himself mindful of man, and the thought of God's greatness, as shown by the heavens, leads him on to praise the great Being who, in spite of all this splendour, has yet time for man, making him but a little lower than the angels, crowning him with glory and honour and giving him dominion over the animal creation. There is here a clear reference to the image of God, which is always in the Bible associated both with glory and the dominion over the animal creation.

Before we pass on to the New Testament it is worth while summing up our conclusions, thus far. Probably the writer of Genesis 1, when he referred to the image and likeness of God in man, merely thought of a certain undefined likeness to God which was the source of human dignity and sacredness. But we may be justified in interpreting this dignity further, not as man's power of reason—though this is a result and symptom of the image—but rather as man's existence as a person. Since personal existence can never be in isolation, man is a person because he is the being to whom God speaks. He is also the being who needs human companionship, as the first man in Genesis did, who was consequently given the companionship of the woman to be a help to him.

When we turn to the New Testament references to the image, we are at once conscious of a certain change in the use of the term, though the general world of thought remains the same as that of the Old Testament. Here, however, the purposes of God have ripened fast, and the most crucial event of history has occurred, the coming and life and death and resurrection of Christ. And it is clear that when the New Testament speaks of the image of God, in the great majority of instances the reference is not to man's humanity which cannot be lost. The main reference is rather to God's purpose for man, to man as

H

God wills that he should be. I have not here the space to discuss the various passages about the image of God in the New Testament. It will be enough to sum up some of the chief points under three headings.

(1) Jesus Christ is himself described as the image of God, or in similar terms, because it is from him that we learn what God is like. When Philip said to him 'Show us the Father' the Fourth Gospel records that Jesus answered 'Have I been so long time with you Philip, and yet you have not known me? He that has seen me has seen the Father.' In Jesus God has revealed himself to us; because we know Jesus, we can trust God implicitly; there is nothing in the Father that is contrary to the Son. Jesus the Son is the 'living image' of the Father, as we say in a common turn of speech.

But the New Testament calls Jesus the image of God for another reason. He is the image of God because he is the perfect man, man as God meant man to be. He trusts and loves the Father absolutely, and wills to have no other will than the Father's. And he loves men perfectly also, and it is his destiny to bring them back to God and to perfect manhood; to give them forgiveness and deliverance from sin and guilt, from meaninglessness and despair. He has opened up the way, and God will accept those who take Jesus as their master; they too can become members of God's family, God's sons, Christ's brothers.

(2) So we pass on to a second sense of the term 'image of God' in the New Testament. Men are destined to become the image of God by fulfilling the glorious destiny God planned for them at the first, which sin has blocked, and Christ has again made possible. There is a very striking and poetic reference made by St. Paul to an

incident of the Old Testament. It is in the third and fourth chapters of his second letter to the Corinthians, and he is referring to a story told in the thirty-fourth chapter of Exodus in the Old Testament. There it is said that Moses went up into the mountain of God and conversed with him, and that when he came down to the plain his face shone, though he did not know it. And when they saw him, his brother Aaron and the rulers of the people were awed by the glory that shone in his face, so that he had to put on a veil to hide it when he was talking to them. It may be that some of us have seen something like this in the faces of people we knew who lived very near God. They were themselves unaware of it, but it silenced criticism, and made us feel that God was near.

Well, says Paul, when Moses came down, he put on a veil over his face to hide the glory of God that was reflected in it, a fading glory that soon left no afterglow. But we Christians behold the glory of Jesus Christ our Lord, and our destiny is to become a reflection of that same glory. That is our high destiny, to become like him who loves us, and whom in return we love.

(3) Now we come to the third point. Jesus is God's image, and we are in our own way destined to become the image also. But it is not just a one-to-one relationship the New Testament is thinking of. We are not only joined to him, so that he is ours and we are his, but we who accept him are thereby all joined to each other in an eternal destiny and bond of love. The New Testament never speaks of me or you being the image of God, but always of *us*. It is true that each man and woman is meant to have an immediate relation to Christ; but at the same time he must be one with the rest of Christ's

disciples. We are the body of Christ, the Church, and to be members of the Church is God's plan for all men and women who are willing to respond to this call. Their destiny begins here on earth, but it stretches beyond into an unknown and glorious future. This is the real purpose and meaning of human nature.

This is a very meagre summary of the Christian teaching about man, but I have said enough to show that it is a message of hope in a dark world. It brings courage in face of danger and discouragement, it brings meaning and satisfaction into life; it gives us the power to trust that the God who has done such wonderful things in the past will not forsake us, or his world, but has a great all-embracing purpose which includes both time and eternity, a purpose of good to all. Can we believe it? If you are puzzled, and want to come to an honest decision, then you must take into account not only the Christian Doctrine of Man, but also the whole of which it is a part, and which I had to draw, in the merest outline, round my meagre sketch of man. And further, belief is not just the acceptance of a view of the world, but a personal commitment to the God who is seeking you. But in this commitment, your mind can't be neglected, and God can bless and guide your mind as well as your will. A man who has accepted Christ also believes that the Christian faith makes a better meaning of life and the world than any other faith.

I said at the beginning that in general, when science and faith seemed to conflict, it was usually because one or other of them was trespassing beyond its real boundaries. I should like in conclusion to refer to one real difficulty which lies in the way of accepting the Christian view of man, and which seems to come from science.

I cannot here deal with it adequately, but I can give one or two reflections about it.

Earlier in this essay I referred to the eighth psalm, which records one man's wonder that the God who created the moon and the stars was yet so kind to man, and had taken thought for him. But the world the ancient Hebrews lived in, or thought they lived in, was a fairly small world, even though they were very aware of its greatness and mystery and glory. They had no conception even of the distance of the moon and its true size, much less of the staggering distances of the stars. But year by year we realize more and more how profound are the abysses of space on every side of us, and we must say, that if indeed it is not limitless, as the astronomers seem today to suggest it is not, then it is so vast that for the ordinary man the fact of its not being infinite makes little difference! And further, the universe is incredibly old, millions of times older than the writer of the eighth psalm knew. The Milky Way which we see like a band of faint light on a dark night spanning the heavens, is a vast cloud of stars which are so many and so distant that we cannot see them separately. It is a flattened disc which rotates about once in 200,000,000 years. And it is so huge, that light, which travels at 186,000 miles per second, takes about 100,000 years to cross from one side of the Milky Way to the other. And this is not all; the heavens are full of other such systems, which are called nebulae, and are seen in telescopes—as tiny patches of light. Some of the biggest of these—that is, the nearest—can be seen by the naked eye on a moonless night. The Nebula in Andromeda is one of these, and is about 680,000 light years away from us. Can the God, or Being, who created this colossal system of

universes have any thought for man? If it was brought
into being for some purpose, how can the growth and the
salvation of the human race have any significant part in
this purpose? Here, it would seem, science leads us on
from questions of fact, which are its true province, to
questions of purpose and meaning, and indeed points
to a philosophy or world-view, and one which is different from the Christian view of man and of the world. It
seems as if we could not help feeling the draught of the
cold wind blowing in upon us from these infinite spaces
and immeasurable ages. No wonder that the great
Christian philosopher and mathematician Pascal said
'The eternal silence of these infinite spaces terrifies me'.

I am not going to try here to give a complete discussion
of these difficulties; but there are one or two considerations I would suggest. The sceptical conclusion is not
the only possible one to draw from the facts of modern
astronomy.

First, science also tells us that in an ordinary poker
which we use to stir the fire, there are as many atoms as
there are stars in our universe, the Milky Way. Man is
thus not only infinitely small in relation to the stellar
distance, he is infinitely large in relation to the atomic
distances. He is in fact about half-way! We might conclude from this that the Creator does not care quite so
much whether things are very large or very small. Size
does not determine value in his eyes. Further, while the
life of a man is only for a tiny second of time compared
with the astronomical ages, yet is it not enough for the
enactment of the drama of his life? May it not be that
in the life of a man or woman things can be achieved
which all the roaring white-hot furnaces of the stars
cannot produce? As Pascal said, Man is a reed, but he

is a reed that thinks, that can know and weigh and measure and chemically analyse this vast universe.

There is another thought that suggests itself. If science has shown the world to be so much vaster in age and extension than the men of old times thought, is that a logical reason for believing that the Creator of it, whom we know, by reason of its immensity, to be so much more powerful and august than men could have guessed, should therefore be *less* glorious in his moral attributes of holiness, justice and love, than men had believed? Would it not be as logical, if not more so, to turn the sceptical argument from the physical immensities on its head?

Thus I am suggesting that the facts of astronomical science are susceptible of more than one interpretation, and that they do not at all inevitably lead us to doubt about God, but may very well fit in with the Christian teaching about him and about man. The Bible never tells us that God has no other interests save man; in fact one of the things that the book of Job impresses on us is the fact that he has. So the Christian and the other interpretations must be set against each other, but none of them can claim that it stems inevitably from the proved facts of experimental science.

In the end, however, we Christians come back to the same point. Our faith is not based on scientific results, but on what we believe to be revelation; in the final issue upon the claims which Jesus makes for himself, and on his assurance that God is our Father, who has forgiven us our sins, and will restore us to the glorious destiny he has planned for us, the destiny of being his sons and daughters now and for ever. That he will watch over us to bless us, and that no misfortune comes to us which cannot be overruled for good if we will trust him. And this also was the conclusion of Pascal who wrote in his diary words that were only discovered after his death. 'God of Abraham, God of Isaac, God of Jacob. Not of the scientists and philosophers. God of Jesus Christ. . . . Thy God shall be my God. . . . I fled him, renounced him, crucified him. May I never be separated from him. He is to be kept only by the ways taught in the Gospel.'

God in History

HERBERT BUTTERFIELD

O F all the factors which have operated to the disadvantage of religion and the undermining of the religious sense in recent centuries, the most damaging has been the notion of an absentee God who might be supposed to have created the universe in the first place, but who is then assumed to have left it to run as a piece of clockwork, so that he is outside our lives, outside history itself, unable to affect the course of things and hidden away from us by an impenetrable screen. This idea has had unfortunate effects upon religion and religious life even within the bosom of the Church itself. It has helped to discourage many people who were not really unfriendly to religion—helped to push them away on to the fringe of Christianity and into the position of friendly neutrals, sitting on the fence, but not quite convinced that there is anything very much that they can do about religion. Some of them believe in God but, since he is an absentee God, shut out from the events of this world, he might as well not be there—one can't really have a deep or a vivid kind of religion in relation to such a God. Indeed such a God does harm by giving people a comfortable general feeling of optimism about the universe, combined with a feeling that there is not very much point in troubling oneself about religion. And if God cannot play a part in life, that is to say, in history, then neither can human beings have very much concern about him or very real relationships with him. Nothing is more important for the cause of religion at the present day than that we should recover the sense and consciousness of the Providence of God—a Providence that acts not merely by a species of remote control but as a living thing, operating in all the details of life—working at every moment, visible in every event. Without this you cannot have any serious religion, any real walking with God, any genuine prayer, any authentic fervour and faith.

It is clear that one of the reasons why people have lost their way in regard to this question is due to the effects of science, the effects of what I should call popular science rather than of the scientific mind or the scientific method as such. Partly this is the result of the fact that men have forgotten how the modern scientific method came into existence and the terms on which it came to be developed —have forgotten just what are the limits of what can be achieved by observing a blade of grass more and more microscopically or by looking at the stars through bigger and bigger telescopes. Partly people are over-awed by the things which we call 'laws of nature', thinking of them as laws in the sense that Acts of Parliament are laws, when rather they are hypotheses—they represent our mode of understanding nature, our ways of formulating to ourselves the movements and processes that we observe to be taking place in the universe. And, if we make a mistake about this, our view of life and the world is apt to be very mechanical. In the old days they would teach musical composition by the use of mechanical rules, and the student had to do exercise after exercise until he had mastered the rules. The rules themselves were all taken from an analysis of the works of successful composers—it was possible to show that on the whole successful music did in fact conform to these particular rules. Everybody knew, however, that the great composers actually writing music never wrote it to rule in this way—the rules were things which you discovered when you subjected good music to mechanical analysis afterwards. It would be a wild error to imagine that the composer created his music in the way in which students analysed it after it had been written. And similarly one must not imagine that God created the universe in the way in which we analyse it—more likely he resembled the composer who, we might say, was just out to create a beautiful thing. Above all one of the effects of this misunderstanding of the scientific method has been to give people a too mechanical and too abstract idea of God—one which fails to do justice to his fullness and richness. In particular we forget those significant words which St. Paul declared to the men of Athens when they, also, were worshipping an unknown God, too remote, too far removed from human life and history. St. Paul said: 'He giveth to all life, and breath, and all things. . . . he is not far from every one of us; for in him we live and move and have our being'. If we grasp those words properly and see all the world lying in the hollow of God's hand—see ourselves as living and moving only in him—then it becomes less difficult to imagine how intimately all Nature and History lie in the Providence of God.

Concerning the events that take place in nature and in history and in life there are three ways that we can have of looking at them—it might be said perhaps that we can imagine them at three different levels and with three different kinds of analysis. And because they are taken at different levels they can all be true at the same time, just as you could have three different shapes of the same piece of wood if you took three different cross-sections. If you go on a journey, and at the end of it I ask: Why are you here now? you may answer: 'Because I wanted to come'; or you may say: 'Because a railway-train carried me here'; or you may say: 'Because it is the will of God'; and all these things may be true at the same time—true on different levels. So with history: we may say at the first level of analysis that men's actions make history—and men have free will—they are responsible for the kind of history that they make. But, then, secondly, at a different level, we find that history, like nature itself, represents a realm of law—its events are in a certain sense reducible to laws. However unpredictable history may be before it has happened it is capable of rational explanation once it has happened; so much so that it becomes difficult sometimes to imagine that it ever had been possible for anything else to have happened or for history to have taken any other course. Now these two things are difficult enough to reconcile in themselves—first of all the free will of human beings and secondly the reign of law in history. But they are reconcilable—and historians can discover large processes taking place in society for a hundred years to produce a French Revolution and an Industrial Revolution; and yet at the same time the historian will treat the French revolutionaries themselves or the nineteenth-century capitalists as subjects of free will, capable of making one decision rather than another, and even blamable for certain decisions that they actually made. We can even work out the laws and conditioning circumstances which have made the twentieth century an epoch of colossal

world-wars; and those laws are so clear that some people
were predicting their ultimate results nearly a hundred
years ago. Some people in the nineteenth century, analysing the processes that were taking place in their time,
predicted that the twentieth century would be a period
of stupendous warfare and of still more prolonged war-
strain. Yet, looking at the story from a different angle,
we do not say that nobody is to blame for the outbreak
of war in Europe in July 1914. The men who made dis-
astrous decisions in July 1914 are still responsible and
blamable for the decisions that they made.

But besides the freedom of the human will and besides
the reign of law in history, there is a further factor that
is operative in life and in the story of the centuries—one
which in a sense includes these two other things—
namely the Providence of God, in whom we live and
move and have our being. And in part the Providence
of God works through these two other things—it is Providence which puts us in a world where we run all the
risks that follow from human free will and responsibility.
It is Providence which puts us into a world that has its
regularities and laws—a world therefore that we can do
something with, provided we learn about the laws and
the regularities of it. It would be wrong for us to picture
God as interfering with the motion of the planets, stop-
ping one of them arbitrarily, hurrying another of them
along by sheer caprice—for we cannot imagine God as
working by mere caprice. Indeed, centuries ago (before
modern science had come into existence) men were looking for the laws and regularities in nature because they
felt sure that God would not act by mere caprice. God
is in all the motion of the planets—just as he is in all the
motions of history. He is not interfering with the stars

in their rotations—he is carrying them round all the time and in him they live and move and have their being. In his Providence he continues the original work of Creation and keeps the stars alight, maintains his world continually; we ought to feel that if he stopped breathing it would vanish into nothingness. It is like the case of the people you see in dreams—when you stop dreaming they no longer exist; and when God stops his work of creating and maintaining this universe we ourselves and all this fine pageantry of stars and planets simply cease to exist any longer. Those people are right who praise God every morning for the rising of the sun, and who see in this not merely a Providence which operated at the creation of the solar system millions of years ago, but evidence of his continuing care, his ever-present activity. It is not meaningless to praise God for the coming of the spring or for bringing us safely through to another day. It is because God is in everything, in every detail of life, that people so easily think that they can cancel him out. The world comes to do its thinking as though he did not exist.

Now that is the real affirmation that we as Christians have to make about life before the world at the present day—a world that is like something derelict and disinherited because it has lost touch with a really present God, with the real immediacy of God. It means that the Providence of God is at work in the downfall of Nazism, in the judgements that come on the British Empire for its own sins, in the present prosperity of the United States, and in our own individual daily experiences. That is what we see with the higher and more royal parts of our minds, when we make our highest judgements about life—our real valuations about events. And that is what we ought to

say when we have our national joys, or our national vic-
tories or our national problems or our national dangers.
We have to say: Providence has put us in this predicament—what can it mean? what moral good can we get out
of it? what does God intend us to do when he puts this
problem before us? what sins did we commit as a nation
to merit this response from God and from history?

For let us make sure of one thing—in the long run
there are only two alternative views about life or about
history. Here is a fact which was realized thousands of
years ago and it is still as true as ever. Either you trace
everything back in the long run to sheer blind Chance,
or you trace everything to God. Some of you might say
that there is a third alternative—namely that everything
just happens through the operation of the laws of nature.
But that is not an explanation at all and the mind cannot
rest there, for such a thesis does not tell us where the laws
themselves can have come from. Either we must say that
there is a mind behind the laws of nature—there is a
God who ordered things in that particular way—or we
must say that in the infinity of time all possible com-
binations of events are exhausted by the blind work of
Chance, which produces amongst all the planets of the
sky at any rate one where vegetation is possible and
where animal life develops, and where in human beings
matter itself acquires the quality of mind. There was one
historian who outshone all others in regarding history
as a science and historical events as subject to law. He
was the Regius Professor of History in my University, a
very famous scholar, Professor Bury, and in his Inaug-
ural Lecture he stated in its most rigid form the scientific view of the course of history. But as he grew older
he became greatly puzzled by the fact that he could

explain why a Prime Minister happened to be walking down a street, and he could explain the scientific laws which loosened a tile on a roof so that it fell down at a particular moment; but he could not explain the conjuncture of the two—the fact that the Prime Minister should just be there to be killed by the falling tile—and yet it was just this *conjuncture* of the two things which was the most important feature of the story. What was more significant still—he found that all history was packed with these conjunctures—you can hardly consider anything in history without coming across them—so that this rigid believer in the firmness of scientific laws in history turned into the arch-prophet of the theory that Chance counted most of all. In his view the whole of the world's history was altered, for example, by the shape of Cleopatra's nose. Similarly he said that the Roman Empire fell in the West because of a handful of separate events which unfortunately happened to be taking place at the same time. Any single one of these events could be explained and reduced to law, but it was their conjuncture that mattered, and this Bury could only account for as the effect of Chance. Indeed when you go on analysing historical events further and further you find that the final problem of all—the really big thing that you have to solve—is this problem of the conjuncture. You can explain why each separate thing happened; but the important thing is the combination—the Prime Minister's path crossing the path of the tile at a given moment. If Hitler had been executed in 1925 or if Churchill had been killed in the Boer War we can be sure that all our history in this present year would have been different, though we should still have been able to work out scientifically the laws which help to explain how things came to happen in that way. Chance itself, or some equivalent of it, seems to have its part to play in historical explanation, therefore. And the historical process is much more subtle and flexible than most people seem to understand.

So, when we are considering historical events, there are three ways in which we can look at them. The first I would call the biographical way—we can see human beings taking their actions and decisions and operating with a certain amount of freedom so that they can be held responsible for the decisions they make; and in this sense men do make their own history and can blame themselves when their history goes wrong. The Christian would always have to be very emphatic about the free will of men and their moral responsibility—more emphatic I believe than anybody else; and he must come to the conclusion that all men are sinners—even all the statesmen of 1914 would have been wiser if they had had less egotism, less fear for their vested interests. The second way of looking at historical events is what I should really call the historical way rather than the biographical one—because it is the scientific examination of the deep forces and tendencies in history—the tendencies for example which had been making for war in Europe for fifty years before 1914, almost before the statesmen of 1914 were born—deep forces and tendencies which were working in fact for generations to help to make the twentieth century an era of colossal warfare. In this sense there is a part of men's history which the men themselves do not make—a history-making that goes on over their heads—helping to produce a French Revolution or an Industrial Revolution or a great war. And in this aspect of history we are much less inclined

I

to blame the human beings concerned, and we see how much we have to be sorry for them. A Christian again must be most emphatic in his demand for this kind of history, this scientific kind of history, which examines the deep processes behind wars and revolutions and even tries to reduce them to law. And here is the great opportunity for Christian charity in history—here is why the Christian has to go over the past making no end of allowances for people—no end of explanations—we might almost say that he cannot read history without being a little sorry for everybody. So you have free will in history, and the statesmen of 1914 are blamable for unloosing the horses of war. But also you have the operation of laws and processes in history; and the statesmen of 1914 are not as blamable as they might have seemed at first sight, perhaps not more blamable than you yourself might have been if you had been in the same historical predicament—perhaps not more blamable than you yourself have often been at moments when the disaster was only reduced because you did not happen to be a statesman responsible for the welfare of millions of people. Thirdly, however, you have to think of another aspect. Either you must say that Chance is one of the greatest factors in history and that the whole of the story is in the last resort the product of blind Chance, or you must say that the whole of it is in the hands of Providence—in him we live and move and have our being—even the free will of men and even the operation of law in history, even these are within Providence itself and under it. But if you say that it is Providence, you must not imagine that Providence can act merely in a chancy and capricious way—Providence is acting in all that part of history which is subject to law as well as in all that part of history which men otherwise tend to attribute to Chance. And if you hold this view, then there is a further way of looking at the war of 1914—you must regard that war as itself a judgement of God on certain evils of our civilization which could not be rooted out in any other way. And if you look at the question in this light you can even discover what those evils actually were. Indeed we know what the moral diseases of the pre-1914 world were, which led to the outbreak of a European war.

Of course it is possible to read history and study the course of centuries without seeing God in the story at all; just as it is possible for men to live their lives in the present day without seeing that God has any part to play. I could not go to people and say that if they studied nearly two thousand years of European history this would be bound to make them Christian; I could not say that such a stretch of history would prove to any impartial person that Providence underlies the whole human drama. You can learn about the ups-and-downs of one state and another in one century and another, you can learn about the rise of vast empires and the growth of big organizations and the evolution of democracy or the development of modern science—and all this will not show you God in history if you have not found God in your daily life. When we seek to know how God is revealed in history we do not make a chart or a diagram of all the centuries and try to show to what future great world-empires are tending or to what end great human organizations are moving. Russia, the United States, England—these are only names on a map, and if we know anything we know that some time in the far future men will be asking what was this thing called England, just as

we ask about Assyria and Tyre and Sidon—some day
the archaeologists will be rummaging amongst the ruins
of London just as we excavate for Nineveh and hunt for
ancient Troy. If we wish to know how God works in
history we shall not find it by looking at the charts of all
the centuries—we have to begin by seeing how God
works in our individual lives and then we expand this on
to the scale of the nation, we project it on to the scale of
mankind. Only those who have brought God home to
themselves in this way will be able to see him at work in
history, and without this we might be tempted to see
history as a tale told by an idiot, a product of blind
Chance. If a great misfortune comes on us we may just
feel how unlucky we are when compared with all our
other friends who had previously seemed to be in a
condition similar to ours. We need not adopt this attitude, however; there are some people who bring their
sins home to themselves and say that this is a chastise-
ment from God; or they say that God is testing them,
trying them in the fire, fitting them for some more important work that he has for them to do. Those who
adopt this view in their individual lives will easily see
that it enlarges and projects itself on to the scale of all
history; it affects our interpretation of national mis-
fortunes as well as private ones. And when we reach this
point in the argument we realize that we are adopting
the biblical interpretation of history.

The way that God reveals himself in history is in fact
the great theme of the Bible itself. And if you want to
ask: 'How does God reveal himself in ordinary secular
history?' then it is exactly this which is the particular
theme of the Old Testament. The Old Testament is the
history of a people whose fate and vicissitudes were un-

commonly like those of most other states—even modern ones. If the history was peculiar, it was perhaps in being worse and more violent than that of other states; for the ancient Hebrews lived in a tiny country with vast empires rising on either side of them and they retained their political independence only for a moment, only for a tiny fraction of their history. Afterwards, down till the twentieth century their land remained under the heel of vast empires, the Assyrian, the Babylonian, the Persian, the Roman, the Arabian, and the Turkish Empire in turn. Where they differed from other nations was in the way in which they interpreted their history—in fact it was their way of interpreting their history that was their chief contribution to the development of civilization. Because of that, they are remembered today and hold a high place in the world's story, even though they were no bigger than Wales and retained their political independence for so short a period.

They saw God as being essentially the God of History, and the result was that first and foremost they regarded history as based on the Promise. And although they took this Promise in a purely nationalistic way, all Christians must regard history as based finally on the Promise—it is never permitted to a Christian to despair of Providence. But the Children of Israel sinned, and theirs is the only national history I ever remember reading which proclaimed the sinfulness of the nation—proclaimed its own nation even to be worse than the other pagan nations round about them. And because of this, history at the second stage of the argument appeared to this people in its aspect as Judgement. When colossal national disaster came upon them they saw the tragedy as the effect of a Judgement from Heaven. At the next stage, however, they

saw that God's Judgement does not cancel his Promise—
if God judged the nation it was only in order to save it—
for God is Love and it is always dangerous to think of
the power of God without also thinking of his love. Even
when their distresses were at their greatest and God
seemed to be chastising them most severely, they came
to what I think is the ultimate picture of God in History
—God looking upon this world of cupidity and cross-
purposes, of violence and of conflict—and pulling upon
it like a magnet—drawing men with his loving-kindness.
Judgement might fall heavily upon them but they were
undefeatable in one respect. They saw that the Judgement did not cancel the Promise.

The Children of Israel had actually come in sight of
the Promised Land—their spies had actually entered it
and brought samples of its rich fruits—when they met
an unexpected enemy whom God told them they must
fight before they could actually enter the Promised Land
—and they rebelled against him for putting them to this
further trial. God brought us out of the land of Egypt
because he hated us, they said—he brought us here only
to entrap us. Let us go back to the land of Egypt, back
to the House of Bondage. Let us make a captain and let
us return to Egypt, they said. And God was so angry
that he said they should not see the Land of Promise—
their carcasses should fall in the wilderness. But in spite
of the Judgement he kept his Promise to the Children of
Israel—for though these people themselves were not to
enter the land of Canaan, he decreed that their children
should come into it later. He did not take hope away
from the world.

And much later than that, when in the days of the
prophets Judgement came upon the Kingdoms that the

Children of Israel had established, and Jerusalem itself was razed to the ground—still once again the Judgement did not cancel the Promise—God said that he would make a new covenant with his people. He said that even his sending them into exile was meant for their further good—and we know that these particular experiences deepened the religion of the Children of Israel in many remarkable ways, so that this period of defeat and anguish was one of their great creative moments. Just at this time they gave a new development to the history of religion and religious thought. It proved to be an immortal moment for them.

But even now they sinned through excessive nationalism and worldly-mindedness, and when God made a new Covenant with them, they took it to mean a promise of new worldly success, victory in war, glory for their kingdom, dominion on earth. After this date the ancient Hebrews committed some terrible and wilful mistakes because they believed that God was to be on their side in battle and was to bring their nation to the top of the world—they even believed that the promised Messiah was to be a warrior-leader, a military saviour. Again their punishment was terrible and tragedy after tragedy came upon their endeavours; but the Judgement did not cancel the Promise. The trouble was that God's Promise to them was a higher thing than they knew, a better thing than they had imagined. They had been construing God's Promise in too worldly a way. And, though they were wrong, the Promise was not cancelled.

The greatest of the Old Testament Jews came to realize that God's Promise was not one of luxury and worldly success—it was a Promise that the nation should have a mission—a mission that should give meaning to its very disasters—and it was through that mission that it was to have a great role in history, an immortal name amongst men. Its mission was to teach the nations of the world about God—to spread to the rest of mankind the special revelation it had had—the knowledge of God as revealed in history. Through the very sufferings of Israel the world was to be carried to a higher religious life. It was the final mark of their mission that Christ was to come into the world as a member of this stricken, oppressed subject-nation—a Messiah who was to bring them greater glory and fame, a greater place in history than any warrior-leader ever could have done. It was a sign of the perpetual blindness and sinfulness of this nation that it rejected the Messiah when the Messiah actually came. That is the history of a nation whose stories of violence and conflict, treachery and war, of worldliness and cupidity, could be told just like the story of any other nation. The one difference was that the ancient Jews interpreted their history differently and saw the hand of God in it—they had the same experiences as other nations but they turned those experiences into spiritual experiences and because of that their history did become different—because of that they achieved creative things. For the greatest triumph of spirit over matter is when people can turn even their defeats and distresses into a creative moment like that.

We must imagine Providence as doing the best that the wilfulness of men allows it to do. For all of us History is the Promise and we need never despair—but it is a Promise punctuated by acts of Judgement. Even the great disasters of history, like the Jewish Exile, or the downfall of the Roman Empire, or the Norman

Conquest of England can turn out to appear in history as a colossal benefit to mankind, and Providence can draw even good out of evil. It can even use our past sins to serve its future purposes. The Judgement of God may come upon an old world only to make way for a new one. Perhaps it is the only way in which on occasion the world in general can be induced to rise higher.

PART III

DOCTRINES OF THE CHRISTIAN FAITH

★

The Person of Jesus Christ

S. P. T. PRIDEAUX

I. THE BACKGROUND

THE ancient world accepted the existence of a spiritual world and of divine beings as axiomatic, and the activities of God, or the gods, as real; but their ideas as to their character and methods were elementary, and often mistaken and wrong.

The Hebrews, under the influence of Moses, Samuel, Elijah and the later prophets, rose out of the primitive level of religion and ethics, and attained gradually to a far higher level than their contemporaries in their ideas and knowledge of God, of his relations with the world of men and things, and of man's relations with him and with man's fellow men. Chastened and disciplined by deportations to Assyria and Babylon in the eighth and the sixth centuries B.C., and challenged by life among heathen peoples elsewhere in the following centuries, the more spiritual element of the nation survived (now known as the Jews) and their religion and ethics were gradually raised and purified. They used and accommodated themselves to the best elements in the contemporary world, although at the same time their outlook was made rigid by an exaggerated devotion to the letter of the Torah (i.e. teaching and customs rather than 'law') handed down from their ancestors.

They believed that the universe had a divine origin; it was not self-existent but had been created by God, and man had been created in order to serve God, and live in personal touch and loving union with him.

Central in their life was the belief that they were a people specially chosen by God to hand on their superior beliefs and way of life to the rest of the world, and that one day he would send a special representative to free them from their enemies and to bring in a universal state of happiness and prosperity. This is the meaning of 'Messiah' (Hebrew = anointed; in Greek, 'Christ'.)

All this is traceable in the Old Testament, a collection of writings due to the prophets and their successors. These men were inspired teachers rather than predictors of future events (as they are often misrepresented), possessing insight rather than foresight, although they did forecast, in general and often varying terms, the coming of the Deliverer.

This is all unique in the world's history; nothing like it has happened before or since; and it is all actual fact and has been largely verified and upheld by ancient records and modern archaeological research.

No less unique are the facts that the development of the Roman and Greek peoples converged at the same time as that of the Jews, in such a way that at the time of the birth of Jesus the Romans were in possession of the then civilized world, giving it order, good government and means of communication; the Greek language was in use everywhere and Greek philosophical thought (still in the twentieth century A.D. regarded with respect and valued) widely known; Jews were to be found in every country and city of importance, making their pagan neighbours familiar with their particular ideals; these Jews were known as 'the Dispersion'. The early religions were becoming discredited; neither philosophy nor the 'mystery religions' were satisfying man's deepest needs; Judaism had reached the limit of its growth and was becoming fossilized. The centre of Judaism was at Jerusalem, a point geographically linking East and West. The whole 'set-up', of time, place and development was exactly what was needed for the particular event to which the Jews were looking forward, and for the wide extension of whatever might be the result of it.

Later generations were so much impressed that they made the birth of Jesus the central point and dividing line in history and reckoned the previous years as 'Before Christ', B.C., and those following it as 'Anno Domini', A.D., 'in the year of the Lord'.

II. JESUS OF NAZARETH

The evidence available—which will be dealt with later—shows that Jesus was really and truly human, a Jew, living a man's life on earth and possessing the ordinary faculties of a man, and also showing the ordinary limitations of human knowledge and of his own time and generation, subject to physical weakness and to moral temptations. At the same time he exercised powers which are unusual, such as healing the sick, freeing people from 'evil spirits' and manias; and it was claimed that he could control the forces of nature and even raise the dead to life. The impact of his personality was still more striking: he had great personal charm; he was an

effective and convincing teacher, using a method different from that of the teachers in his day and challenging
much of what they taught; he was masterful in his ways
with men and knew no fear; he commanded and men
obeyed; in character no fault could be seen in him, he
was entirely innocent of evil, without any moral defect
or weakness, reckoned as sinless and perfect; he 'went
about doing good' and winning a wide response. With
the sinful he had great sympathy and was always ready
to help those who showed the least sign of remorse, but
to the self-righteous, especially those who had had full
spiritual opportunities, he was unsparingly severe.

More remarkably, he claimed to be the promised deliverer, the Messiah, a claim which implied deity, to be
'Son of God'; he claimed the right of judging men and
of forgiving their sins; and with all these stupendous
powers and claims he gave the impression of being perfectly stable and well-balanced, sane, consistent and
honest, and not in the least weighed down by the burden
of such claims and the responsibility of them, or by any
sense of unworthiness.

This claim was accepted by some of his contemporaries
but not by the religious leaders, who trumped up a
charge against him and persuaded the Roman authorities
to execute him as a common criminal, by crucifixion.

In his teaching Jesus upheld that of the Hebrew
prophets, that there is one God only, who originated the
universe, sustains and controls all the processes and
activities in it; God is morally holy and upright, hating
all forms of evil; at the same time he is merciful to the
weak and restores those who repent of their wrongdoing
or sin. God stands to man as father to child, loves and
provides for him and is always approachable. But, and

here he adds a new truth, God even goes out of his way
to help man and free him from evil.

About man Christ upheld the Old Testament teaching
and ideals: man's divine origin and destiny and his religious and ethical obligations; his free will; his failure
to live up to the standard set before him, and his moral
weakness, his sins against God and his fellow men.

About himself he spoke of his being God's Son in a
special and unique manner, and he claimed, by both
word and act, to be the promised Deliverer. All through
his life he thought of God as working in and through
him and that the purpose of his life was to do God's will.
The prophets and their successors had pictured the
Messiah (= anointed one) under the various figures of
king (from David's line and the tribe of Judah), warrior,
judge, shepherd, priest, prophet, God's servant, a
'chosen one'; they had described him as righteous, pure
from sin, wise, meek, as human and also as divine, pre-
existent; one writer saw that he would have to suffer in
his work of deliverance; and it is remarkable that all
these elements have a place in the person of Jesus, and
to them must be added the notion of the divine Wisdom
which appears in writers after 300 B.C.; and that of the
Logos or Word, a name with links in both Jewish and
Greek thought, and now the equivalent of a 'special
message', 'something which God had to say'. As to the
suffering, he realized that it was inevitable and that it
was by the way of suffering and death that man's
deliverance was to be effected; but he claimed that his
death would not be the end but a beginning, and that he
would return from death having conquered the power
of evil. At some future date there would be a judgement when all men would be called to account for

their lives, and he would be the judge, acting for and as God.

The general impression made on his contemporaries was that not only was he a man very much out of the ordinary but that, in a way unknown to and unexplainable by them, he possessed divine powers and shared the very nature of God himself. This was the conviction of the small band of men who were his chosen and intimate companions and co-workers. It came to them gradually, and was the result of their experience of his personal holiness and moral perfection—he actually embodied his own ideals; of his power over nature and disease and evil spirits; of his teaching about God and man, its convincingness as to its truth and as the solution of life's problems and difficulties; of his embodying and realizing in himself what the Old Testament prophets had forecast about the Messiah; of their own acceptance by him in spite of their own unworthiness and sinfulness, and of the moral and spiritual power which he gave them. Their conviction was clinched by his reappearances among them after his death, by his visible return to the spirit-world, and by the possession of them ten days later by his personal Spirit on the feast of Pentecost.

The evidence for this is in the New Testament. The first three Gospels give us the main facts of what Jesus was and did and taught, and the fourth adds a commentary and interpretation of it all made a generation later in the light of a life of prayer and meditation, service and suffering, and enriched by and harmonized with the best Greek thought of the day. (Read in a modern translation like that by J. B. Phillips these books show how the first readers would have understood them.)

These four books have been subjected to the severest

criticism and testing and the general truth of the picture
has survived the test. None of these books are bio-
graphies of Jesus in the usual sense; they record the
impressions made by him and by what he said and did
and suffered. The historicity, the factual nature, of the
story has been upheld; it is definitely no myth, and this
actuality tells heavily in support of what the writers
assert about and claim for Jesus. It can even be main-
tained that the very limitation of biographical details
together with the later impact on history prove the
reality and the transcendence of Jesus.

The later impact on history—this is as important and
essential as is the record about Jesus himself and not to
be separated from it. For his followers were convinced
that he had returned from death, passed through it, not
only not destroyed or held by it but possessing even
more vigour and power than before; that he had also
gone back to the spirit-world, to God; and that his
Spirit had been given to them to take the place of his
bodily presence. In this belief and with unmistakable
actuality they healed the sick, both bodily and mentally;
taught wherever they could all that they knew about
Jesus; collected an increasing number of converts (men
and women hitherto heathen in religion and often of
indifferent and morally evil life, and some from their
own Jewish people), this community being known as the
Church. The story begins with the rest of the books of
the New Testament and there is no way of disproving it.

The story is continued. The Church and the Christian
belief and way of life established itself throughout the
known world. It survives all attempts made by both the
Jewish and the Roman authorities to suppress and
destroy it; men and women suffer the loss of property

K

and place, accept torture and death, rather than deny it.
It survives many internal weaknesses and defects, such
as are evident even from the New Testament. It outlives
pagan religion and takes its place; it takes the best of
pagan thought and philosophy and adapts it to its own
use without surrendering anything of its own essence.
It gradually raises the standard of morals, of ethics;
influences the policies of peoples and their rulers; en-
courages philanthropy; develops and extends education;
inspires leading poets, painters, architects, musicians.
All this can be verified from history, often by the eye,
and the movement still goes on, recovering from peri-
odical assaults by persecutors and enemies, by thinkers
and controversialists, from times of spiritual deadness
and moral decay. Men and women, of all ages, races,
temperaments, qualifications, experience, ranks and
orders, find in Jesus the answer to their questions, the
stimulus to moral endeavour, release from the guilt and
slavery of sin, the source of moral and spiritual power,
and foundation of hope. Christianity, the faith and religion based upon the person of Jesus, vitalized still by
him, may be relatively old; at the same time it is ever
young, vigorous and active, its very age upholding its
claim to truth.

III. HOW IS JESUS TO BE EXPLAINED?

We have had the facts, in broad outline, and they call
for explanation and interpretation; there must be some
reason for them, some meaning and purpose in them, i.e.
as long as we believe that this world and its happenings
are rational and purposeful. (There are times, it is true,
when some think the opposite and see no rhyme or reason
in anything, but in spite of much disorder and inter-

ference most people still hold to reason and purpose and feel that did they not operate life would not be liveable.)

From the first there was some interpretation. Jesus's followers had to explain him to themselves and to one another and to their fellow men and women, and their leaders, the apostles, gradually formulated their ideas. In the letters written by St. Paul, St. Peter, St. James and St. John, and the unknown writer of the letter to 'the Hebrews', and in the Sermons recorded in the Acts of the Apostles, these ideas can be seen. Some of them were tentative, elementary, not always fully thought out and not put together in any formal statement, but were expressions of a real conviction and a basic guide to life. These beliefs are known as the Church's 'doctrine', which is a Latin word and means 'teaching', i.e. what the first preachers taught to those who wished to become Christians and become members of the Church.

There is also some 'doctrine' in the Gospels, for the first three were written largely for the instruction of believers, and the incidents and the sayings of Jesus were chosen in order to illustrate and uphold the Church's beliefs about him; the fourth Gospel had a similar purpose, only it was written partly for unbelievers as well and it contains a good deal more reasoned teaching or doctrine.

In the generations which followed the New Testament times, when the Church was more widely and firmly established, when the first excitement and the all-absorbing missionary activities had to some extent slackened, when men had more leisure to think, and when both inquirers and opponents became more numerous and more insistent, much thinking and formulation of beliefs was done. This involved much argument and controversy, often wearisome and not always edifying or to the credit of either side. Bit by bit certain 'heresies' appeared, i.e. beliefs about Jesus which in the judgement of the Church leaders either overstepped the bounds of truth or failed to do justice to all aspects of truth, exaggerated either the divine or the human side of Jesus at the expense of the other. These took the names of the men who put them forward, and from time to time a central council was held and attended by the bishops in order to discuss them and say whether they were to be accepted or condemned. Thus Arius underestimated and denied the full Godhead or deity of Jesus (Council of Nicea, 325); Apollinaris underestimated and denied his full humanity (Council of Constantinople, 381); Nestorius asserted that he was two persons (Council of Ephesus, 431); Eutyches denied that he had two separate 'natures'[1] (Council of Chalcedon, 451).

As a result of these long controversies and discussions a number of statements were drawn up, one after the other, and issued authoritatively by the Church as to what men were to believe; these are known as Creeds. Eventually three only remained, known as the 'Apostles'', the 'Nicene' and the 'Athanasian' creeds respectively. Their purpose was to maintain facts rather than to interpret them, to rule out error and to preserve the belief as to the fact and the nature of God, the deity ('god-ness') as well as the human reality and the work of Jesus known as the Christ,[2] and the being and work of the Holy Spirit in the Church.

[1] On 'nature' and 'person' in this connection see pp. 140 and 160.
[2] It should be noted that 'Jesus' is a personal name, and (as explained above, p. 124) 'Christ' is a title, denoting his character and work; the difference is seen clearly by comparing 'George King' with 'King George'.

While the ideas of the Creeds are based on the New Testament their language is different, and this is due to the fact that men's thoughts and experiences are always changing; fresh aspects of truth appear, and in order to relate these to fundamental truths, fresh words and thought-forms have to be invented. The formulating of the Creeds was spread over several centuries and was carried out by men of different races and backgrounds from the first-century Palestinian authors of the New Testament. This process continues and must continue all down the ages, and the initial facts and ideas have to be re-presented and re-interpreted and adjusted to the needs, experiences and outlook of each generation. This is no easy matter, and further difficulties are added by the way in which the use and the meaning of words themselves change; e.g. 'person' in the Creeds does not mean 'a personality or personal being' so much as 'an impersonation'[1]; for 'substance' we should today use 'reality' or 'essence' (even 'pattern' has been suggested): the Greek *ousia* does not mean 'substance' but essence, 'that by which a thing is itself'; 'almighty' means 'all-controlling' rather than 'all-powerful'; 'hell' is the world of those who have died, not a place of punishment and torment; 'quick' means 'living' and not 'speedy'. Further complications arose from the fact that the Jews thought in concrete practical terms and not in abstractions like the Greeks; they approached life with an awareness of God while the Greeks looked at it from man's point of view; the Jew believed in a revelation from God while the Greek trusted and used his own reason, and all the discussion took place when men's thoughts were governed by Greek philosophy and, like the New Testament,

[1] See also Dr. Dillistone's remarks in the next chapter, pp. 160–162.

they were expressed in the Greek language; these two opposing ways of thinking had to be brought into some sort of harmony. Latin was also used and this adds to our difficulties; and since then each nation has made its own translation of the originals.

(It is worth noting that many of our difficulties about religion arise from our learning it in the Jewish way; later we are taught to use our minds in the Greek way, and the two attitudes clash and are not easily harmonized.)

It is not only that language is not capable of expressing ultimate realities (the subject of metaphysics, i.e. the 'theory of being and knowing', the study of what lies behind the material or 'natural' in life); but the picture-language so often used—metaphors, analogies—while often very helpful as it gives life and semblance to what is otherwise dry and meaningless, nevertheless fails to represent the whole truth; it may even distort it. (See below, pp. 135, 148.)

Technically, the traditional word used to explain Jesus's coming into the world is 'Incarnation', i.e. Latin for coming or being born in human flesh, as a man—we might translate it 'embodiment'. By it we mean that in the real and actual person, Jesus of Nazareth, the eternal, supreme Being, whom we call God, took a material human form and in it lived and acted and expressed and made himself known, on this earth; an act which bridged and unified both the 'transcendent' and the 'immanent'. Some indication has already been given as to how this belief was reached and of the ways in which men have tried to explain it in the past. How can we now explain, justify and apply it in the light of our own present-day experiences, thought-forms and language, remembering not only the inadequacy of language and metaphor, but that both our knowledge and our experience are still incomplete?

There are two ways of approach: our Greek-trained minds demand a theory, an intellectual explanation, and our selves (which include other faculties besides that of mind and reason) nourished by Jewish and Christian religion require something fuller, deeper and more all-inclusive. Let us take the first demand first.

A priori, if there be a God, and if God and man are in any way related, an incarnation is at least probable, if not necessary, for full and complete union between the two.

If God reveals himself through the natural world, the material universe, an incarnation is both probable and necessary, for man is part of the natural world, with a material body, and he needs a revelation of God in human, personal terms.

If the life of the universe is conducted by the method of evolution, then an incarnation is a not inconsistent and necessary climax.

Jesus satisfies these conditions.

But man also needs a revelation which shall be moral, in agreement with the eternal principles of right and wrong, and a revelation which shall also help him to uphold and cling to the right and to oppose and overcome evil.

The person of Jesus, like everything and everybody else, can only be explained in the light of his purpose, and this was two-fold: to teach and to set free. Men's ideas about God were limited and distorted, and men's lives were spoiled and largely under the power of evil. Jesus came to give fuller and purer knowledge of God, and to break the power of evil (which includes moral

evil or sin) and to free men from it, and from the frus-
tration which it brings. Jesus, in his own person and life,
showed the world what God was like. God was not a
remote, distant being, uninterested and only occasion-
ally active in man's affairs, and then uncertainly and
capriciously. On the contrary he was deeply interested,
ever present and active, kindly disposed and anxious for
man's well being. He was more than Power or Force,
though all things were under his control and purpose;
his actions were governed by wisdom and by right
principle; in himself he was without evil, morally holy;
his relation to men was that of a father to his children,
and his character was summed up in the word 'Love'.
God's care and love for man had now shown itself by
his coming among men in human form, in the person of
Jesus. In his compassion for man, in the grip of suffering and of sin, God had come to save men and to put
right what was wrong.

This brings us to the question of evil.

No one knows what evil is or can say how it originated.
The traditional teaching is given in Genesis 3, the story
of Adam and Eve and the 'fall'—call it legend, folklore,
as you like.[1] There must have been at least one first pair
who emerged from the brute stage and learned the difference between right and wrong, made a wrong choice,
and suffered as the result. 'Fall' is a word which ought
not to have been used, as it suggests falling from a pin-
nacle of perfection which was not what happened; it is
not used in the Bible or by many of the earlier Christian
writers; it would be better to speak of taking a wrong
turn, a perversion, a misuse, a wrong development, a

[1] On the setting of this story in Genesis, see Professor Hooke's
chapter, p. 38.

failure to advance in the right direction. But evil, sin, are facts, only too obvious and real, and the Genesis story is perfectly true in principle, in its moral and spiritual teaching, and man's need of 'salvation' only too evident. And not only man; the rest of the created world is infected with evil; there is suffering and distortion in 'nature' and doubtless in the rest of this vast universe. Jesus has a 'cosmic' status; coming from God the Creator, and as God's agent in creation and in the maintenance of its life, he frees it from evil and brings in a 'new creation'. This was realized by both Isaiah and St. Paul.

From the first men had tried to know and to understand God, and to get the upper hand of evil, and some few, here and there, had reached a comparatively high standard of knowledge and of holiness; but human powers had reached their limit and man as a whole was troubled and enslaved bodily, mentally, morally and spiritually; he suffered from pain, disease and weakness; from wrong thoughts, error, ignorance, falsehood and grief; from bad habit and the power of sin, and on his conscience lay the increasing burden of remorse, a feeling of guilt and offence against a somebody or something. Of this he could not rid himself; he felt that on him as the offender lay the obligation; he needed 'absolution', to be set free from the power of sin, and 'remission', to be relieved of its guilt; and the situation was such that something had to be done which he must do but could not, which only God had the power to do but had neither the obligation nor the right to do. The only way was to effect a combination of God's ability with man's responsibility and this is what Jesus implied, what his followers believed and the Church has ever since taught; 'God was in Christ', 'who for us men and for our salvation came down from heaven and was incarnate—and was made man'.

God, presumably, could have removed physical, material evils by the direct use of his supreme power; but this would have been a radical interference with the observable natural process which appears to be his usual way of working. He could have removed mental evils in the same way, but this would have overridden man's co-operation. The existing order of things, the world as it was, had to be put right, and it was at least more fitting that this should be done from within than from without; a fresh world, had God wished for one, would not have been the same world, and it would have involved the destruction, not the salvation, of the old world. Man deserved some consideration for his efforts to resist and to remove evil; neither the race nor individuals were entirely depraved.

Evil in its three forms needed to be overcome, and proof brought to God that man had repudiated evil. This the race as a whole was neither able nor willing to do; but it could be done by a representative, by a man who, with the power of God, overcame all temptations, was proof against all forms of evil, lived a perfect life, a life entirely devoted and consecrated to good, to doing God's will, which was the purpose of man's being created.

On the face of it there were four ways by which such a man could have been produced:

(i) God could have taken a man born in the usual way; but men so produced had been tried and found wanting, and every new child had some 'taint' of sin, some moral weakness and imperfection (this is what is meant by 'original' sin; the 'entail' of sin had somehow to be broken.

(ii) God could, presumably, have created a new man altogether; but then he would not have been a true representative, not 'one of us'; such a man could have given us no encouragement or help in our struggles against evil; a fresh 'creation' would have been not in accordance with God's usual evolutionary method.

(iii) Such a man might have had a human father and a divine mother, only this will not bear thinking about, and is out of keeping with and wholly contrary to all the evidence which clearly exists.

(iv) God could choose a woman, the best of her kind, and by a direct spiritual intervention play the part of a human father. Here, of course, we come up against a great mystery, which the Church has always taught as such, but if we cannot fully comprehend it we can see much in its favour. It is the most congruous and fitting of all the four possible ways, and avoids their difficulties. It preserves the initiative for God, and he is already spoken of as 'Father' and the source, through his Spirit, of all life and power. True, the intervention involved some departure from the natural order, but some departure was needed and this was the best possible.

Sin has been called the most irrational thing in the universe and it should not surprise us if a unique remedy was called for. By this means God could choose the mother, and prepare her, morally and spiritually, before-hand. Being human she would naturally inherit the 'taint' of sin, but we may think that God's presence would purge this from her and from the child whom she was to bear. This method, from a human mother by a divine act, ensures the fullness and perfection of God's power, the completeness of human nature and its meeting with evil of all kinds, including temptation; Jesus, so begotten and born, could be the 'only Son' of God ('only-begotten' means unique), and man's true representative, 'perfect God and perfect man', with two 'natures' in one 'person', without 'confusion, change, division or severance.'[1] Jesus was 'man' not 'a man'; his *ego*, personality, was divine, pre-existent, clothing itself and operating in a human body; he 'came into history, not out of it'; he was God in and working through man, not a man raised to the divine level. His manhood was full and complete, he was fully 'integrated', even if subject to the limitations of a Jew of his age and place. He was fully representative of both the divine and the human, showing us 'what God is like and what we ought to be like'.

The foregoing may strike us as dry and academic, and abstruse. That is the result of our approach, that of the Greek mind, with its curiosity, for ever asking 'why' and 'how', and leaving on one side other considerations and factors, and it is time to bring in these.

Evil is not so much a problem to be solved as an enemy to be overcome; when you are ill you want to be cured, not to hear a learned description of why and how you are ill. We, each and all of us, the whole race of man, suffer in body, mind and soul; we are all under the condemnation and the power of sin. Evil causes division, oppositions: in our bodies it brings unease, 'dis-ease', and failure of power; in our minds are contradictions, divided aims, even split personality and lunacy;

[1] A quotation from the doctrinal decision of the Council of Chalcedon (compare p. 132 above).

our inmost souls are distressed by spiritual conflict and suffering. We call ourselves 'individuals' but we are divided all the time; we are not 'integers' but 'vulgar fractions'. Human society is divided into many rival groups. Man, by going against God, by doing wrong, by disobedience, has cut himself off from God; by wrong choices and aims, and misuse of their wills, men go on causing antagonisms and disunion, and much conse-quent distress, material and spiritual. The bulk of men have accepted the situation unintelligently and despair-ingly, making what best they could of a bad job; the few who have realized how matters lie do what they can to reduce and remove the evil, but know their own weak-ness and inability. Things have gone wrong and we cannot put them right.

To repeat, something has to be done which man must do (because he is morally responsible for what he has done wrong) yet only God has the power to do. Jesus, in the capacity of the Christ (= chosen deliverer) and as God-man, has done it. This is called technically the 'Atonement', a word which has caused much perplexity but which is understood quite simply if spelt and pro-nounced 'at-one-ment', i.e. making at one. (This is good Shakespeare: see *Othello* IV.i.) Jesus all through his life showed himself master of evil. In its acutest and most violent form he met it at his crucifixion and surrendered his body to it; but in mind and spirit he was not over-come by it; his personality was not destroyed, and by reappearing the third day after his death he showed that not only was he master of death but his body was raised to a greater degree of power than before. In a luminous phrase (that of Professor L. Hodgson), he had 'absorbed and neutralized the power of evil'; 'Death's mightiest powers had done their worst'. Jesus broke the power of evil.

Jesus was the only perfectly 'integrated' person that the world has seen, perfectly 'at one' in himself, morally holy and innocent, entirely consecrated to good and truth, whole-hearted in his devotion to God, governed entirely by love. Man, as an individual, had been 'at-oned', 'adjusted' (i.e. his balance and proportion and make-up corrected) 'justified', quite simply, 'put right'. And all other individuals can be and are 'at-oned', 'put right', when they turn from evil, surrender themselves to Jesus Christ, follow his example and teaching and the direction of his Spirit (the 'Holy Spirit'), and for this they receive the necessary power through the Church and its Sacraments. Opposition and temptation continue, but the inner conflict has been resolved because of the 'indwelling Christ', and by 'dwelling in Christ'.

By the same means man collectively is being 'atoned'. As individuals become Christian and are possessed by and dwelt in by the Spirit of Jesus Christ, the tone and ways of life in the social order are gradually improved and cleared of evil. Individual Christians taken together form a community called the Church (and they call it the 'Body of Christ' because it is the organism by which the Christ is now still at work on earth among men),[1] and it is a fact of history that wherever the Church has been established it has progressively reduced social evils and purged society, lessened war and oppression, helped races and groups to live in peace and mutual help. By the preaching and the example of love the world is being 'put right'.

[1] See also Dr. Dillistone's words on the Body of Christ, p. 157.

A deeper and more difficult matter is the relation between man and God. The severance between the two had been caused by man having wrong ideas about God, and we have seen how these were 'put right' by Jesus Christ, how man's fears and suspicions were thereby removed, and free and open relations were made possible. But the great stumbling-block of sin remained, and all the more when it was realized that all wrongdoing had been done not only against law and principle, but against a Being who was all-loving. Man, by his disobedience and opposition, had alienated himself from God and destroyed the free and open relation which a child should have with his parent, and only when a child says 'I am sorry and I won't do it again' can the situation be put right. God was not angry, resentful and revengeful, anxious to punish man; but God on principle cannot ignore wrong, sin must be made an example of and a penalty exacted; and he needs an assurance of right conduct in the future. And this man could not give, even when anxious to do so, but Jesus, as Son of God and Son of Man, i.e., with God's power and as representing all men, the 'Second Adam', both could and did. He showed to God that there was one member of the race who had repudiated evil and was entirely consecrated to good and to the doing of God's will. This was proved by his life of perfect obedience; the at-one-ing began with his birth and was continued all through his life; it came to its climax on Calvary, by his willingness to die, by the sacrifice of himself, a sacrifice which God could accept on behalf of us all. In religion all the world over sacrifice has been the means by which evil has been countered; the shedding of blood has been regarded as the release of life, and the offering of a victim as the means of releasing God's forgiveness. The victim was a substitute for the offerer, but Jesus as man was himself the offering; by identifying himself with sin and the 'curse' properly laid on it, he judged and condemned it; he also expiated it and removed its guilt, accepting the punishment due to it; he was the 'lamb' which 'took away the sin of the world'.

Jesus, 'at one' in himself, 'at one' with God, put us back into the right relation with God, 'at-oned' us with God. Guilt was taken away, the power of evil broken, and power to do and to be good made available for us. We have to align ourselves with Jesus Christ, claim this power through him, resist and fight against evil and so make and keep effective our 'at-one-ment'.

All this is difficult to understand, and unhappily other difficulties have been brought in to complicate our attempt to understand the matter. These other difficulties can be removed if we realize that—

(a) we should not say 'atone for sin'. We 'expiate' sin; we 'at-one' persons;

(b) our ideas about God are often hazy, limited and mistaken. He is not someone who can be bribed and bought off. The 'at-one-ment' was not a commercial transaction a 'ransom' or a 'price' paid to God, still less to the devil.

It was not a mechanical process, the 'opening of a gate', the giving of a 'free ticket'.

It was not a legal transaction, an abstraction, a quibble or a fiction.

God is not a super-magistrate, a C.I.D. man, anxious to get a conviction and to punish, content even if the victim is entirely innocent.

God is not like some eastern potentate out of the *Arabian Nights*, ill-tempered and spiteful, wanting to revenge himself for his wounded pride and honour.

God does not wish or need to be 'propitiated', put in a good temper. The Bible word so translated does not mean what we mean by 'propitiate'; in the Bible it is sin which is 'propitiated', i.e., wiped out.

God is what Jesus showed him to be, perfect goodness, right and truth, his love wounded by man's sin and grieving over it, but anxious to save him and to bring back his son into the full atmosphere of 'home'. This Jesus made clear in his parables of the Prodigal Son and the Lost Sheep and the Lost Coin.

It was not God who needed to be reconciled to man, but man to God, man's attitude which needed to be changed. 'God was in Christ reconciling the world unto Himself' (2 Corinthians 5:19). He, himself, in love and compassion and that his own purposes might not be defeated, came to win man back and to restore the harmony, the oneness broken by sin; to conquer and remove the evil which was spoiling man's life; he at-oned and at-ones us by his own example, his teaching, his self-sacrifice, and by the power to live a new life.

Of this the Cross is the symbol and the effecting symbol, an act as well as an idea. The Crucifixion was not merely a brutal, degrading, tragic and pathetic event; it was more than a heroic gesture on the part of Jesus, making a strong moral appeal. It was God himself actually at work, carrying out a supreme act of love, giving himself and 'going all out' to help and to set free, re-creating what he had originated, facing and defeating evil. Jesus Christ survived all the attacks made on him; he was proof against all forms of evil. He transformed suffering and gave us power to rise above it, if we treat it as a discipline, a purging, as an opportunity of bearing witness and so using it and mastering it. By rising the third day from the grave and in a higher degree of life he set us free from death and the fear of death, showing that the material and physical are temporary and that the only ultimately real elements belong to the moral and spiritual order.

The Cross is the permanent symbol, and the effecting symbol, of the whole situation and process. A cross is formed by two lines, each going opposite ways; man has got 'across' God, and 'across' his fellow men, by doing wrong; we get 'cross' with one another and with ourselves; the whole of life is 'criss-cross', a mass of innumerable conflicts. The upright symbolizes man's idealism, his wish to do right; the bar is heavy and drags him down. Lay the cross flat and it suggests a straight road, but barred and with side-tracks taking man from his true objective. The Cross showed up the malignity and devastating properties or nature of evil and sin; it also showed what God was like and could do; for on the Cross Jesus Christ defeated evil, put the seal, so to speak, on a perfect life, offered his perfect life to God, satisfied the eternal principle of right, restored the oneness (union) between man and God, and made perfection possible for all through his Spirit, in the Church.

For the Cross was not the end; by his return from death Jesus showed the truth of his claims and teaching and the fullness of his power. Admittedly, it was against all our experience, as was his birth; but the situation was unique, he himself was unique, without parallel, and for such person and situation a unique entry into and a unique ending to life would be both fitting and necessary.

That perfection has not yet been reached is obvious, and for two reasons: only a small proportion of men and women have taken advantage of what Christianity offers, and many of these not as fully or wholeheartedly as they should; also the historical time-sequence is still in being (due in part to God's forbearance, and to his purposes as yet unknown to us); 'the end is not yet'. But as we have seen (p. 142) the world has been largely relieved of much of its evils through the work of the Church, and the issue has been decided; and, just as we may say with truth that Germany lost the Second World War when she invaded Russia, or at the Battle of Britain, although final victory took the allied nations some years to achieve, so evil's back has been broken and its final defeat waits and depends upon man's co-operation.

CONCLUSION

It should be clear now that explanation of the person of Jesus is not all that is called for or is necessary; there are other factors to be allowed for and reckoned with. Metaphysics is not the only category; man consists of more than reasoning power. The moral element has its place in man's make-up, also personal relationships; there is the sense of moral responsibility, involving a judgement sometimes; there is the 'I and you' awareness as between man and man, and between man and the eternal Being he calls God. These things can be described but no description can ever express what friendship between two persons actually is and means to them. Man is a creature living in two worlds or spheres, time and eternity; and eternity, while it includes time, is more than everlastingness; it is of a different order from time, beyond the capacity of measure, and includes ultimate truth and perfection. But while his inner self may be in or close to 'heaven', man's feet are upon earth, and life has to be lived and evil dealt with. Man uses his reason to explain it if he can; his conscience tells him his obligations; he needs 'faith' to lay hold on the eternal verities and make effective his fellowship and unity with the God who made him and his world. God is more than a definition or a formula, an intellectual abstraction; he is more than all that can be said about him; he is a personal, and supra-personal, Being, very much concerned with us. Two words sum up the Christian belief and practice: Life, and Love; and Jesus, as the link between time and eternity, has shown us what God is like, and what we ought to be like; he has given us the ideal picture of individual life and of mutual, social life, and no higher ethical teaching has been or could be offered to us. He has defeated evil and made perfect goodness, in all things, possible to us. Many categories and figures of speech have been used to describe him and his work and the Christian belief and practice; 'life' is the fullest and most all-inclusive and the least misleading.

Mystery remains, inevitably; the person of Jesus Christ is a paradox, as the whole of Christianity is a paradox. The evidence about him leads to the conclusion of God and man fully united in one person; as in the discussions of many other matters there is a tension, a polarity, and the answer is often given as 'either—or', whereas the true answer is 'neither, because both'.

> Wit hath wonder and kind he can
> How maiden is mother and God is man;
> Leave thy asking and believe that wonder
> For might hath mastery and skill goeth under.

Yet if no answer can be given as to 'how', the 'why' remains; if man's curiosity cannot be satisfied, his inmost self is challenged, the personal impact of Jesus is not to be dodged:

> ... those strong Feet that followed, followed after.
>   But with unhurrying chase,
>   And unperturbèd pace,
> Deliberate speed, majestic instancy,
>   They beat—and a Voice beat
>   More instant than the Feet.

G. K. Chesterton has somewhere a story of a man who hated the Cross and tried to run away from it, but as he looked up from his book the Cross faced him from between the window panes. As he left his room he saw it on the panels of his door. He rushed down the street only to come to cross-roads and a finger-post raising its arms like a cross in front of him.

We have to come to terms with Jesus, and this means accepting his; he may not answer our questions, but we have to answer his.

The Holy Spirit

F. W. DILLISTONE

I believe in the Holy Ghost.—THE APOSTLES' CREED

How strange this confession seems when we first examine it! What is the word 'ghost' doing in a Creed of the Church? Does not 'ghost' stand for something rather frightening, half real and half imaginary, something only dimly sensed and quite unpredictable in its behaviour? If, however, we look into the origin and meaning of the word, we find that it is the exact equivalent of 'spirit': the only difference is that the words are derived from two separate families of languages. But then is not the word 'spirit' one which also makes us vaguely uneasy? Does it not call to mind something comparable to the experience of Eliphaz, the Temanite, in the Book of Job?

> Now a thing was secretly brought to me, and mine ear received a little thereof.
> Then a spirit passed before my face; the hair of my flesh stood up:
> It stood still, but I could not discern the form thereof: an image was before mine eyes, there was silence and I heard a voice.

There is little doubt that these are the associations all too commonly attached to the words 'ghost' and 'spirit', and for this reason alone it is far from easy to make clear what is the Christian Faith concerning the Holy Ghost or Holy Spirit.

Perhaps the best way to begin is to look again at the

word 'spirit' and inquire more closely about its origin. We find that it has come into English from the Latin word *spiritus* which *can* mean spirit but also stands both for 'wind' and 'breath'. We can go further and ask what was the situation in Greek. There we discover that the word *pneuma* (which has given us our word 'pneumatic') can likewise stand for 'spirit' or 'wind' or 'breath'. Strangely enough, exactly the same is true in the Hebrew language. Thus in all three of the languages which played so prominent a part in the history of early Christianity, 'spirit' is closely linked either with the wind which blows down from the mountains and in from the ocean or with the breath which fills our lungs and animates our bodies. Somehow the action of spirit is akin both to that of the wind which operates in our external world and to that of the breath which operates in the inner framework of our bodies.

Now let us turn to the Old Testament and see how men used this kind of language when they were speaking of *God's* activities in human life. Sometimes when the wind came sweeping down the mountain gorges and stirring everything to new life, they said, 'That is God's breath'. Or when a man, exhausted through some unusual expenditure of energy, gulped a draught of fresh air into his lungs, he said, 'That is God's breath'. Or yet again when there came some new impulse to go forward along the paths of righteousness and peace, some said, 'That is God's breath'.

Often in the Old Testament it is hard to be sure whether the word which is used represents what we should call 'physical' breath, or whether it stands for some more mysterious influence operating in what we should call the 'spiritual' world. The fact is that the

Hebrews made no such clear-cut distinctions between the 'physical' and 'spiritual' as we are accustomed to do. To them it was enough to say that the 'breath' or the 'spirit' of the Lord was at work, creating, sustaining, empowering, renewing. 'Breath' and 'wind' were the most vivid images that they could find to describe the altogether powerful yet altogether beneficent activities of the God whom they worshipped and served.

Generally speaking, then, we may say that the Bible uses the terms 'the Spirit of God' or 'the Spirit of the Lord' to represent God in action in human life. No phenomena of the natural world seemed so apt to describe the nature of these activities as did the stirring of the wind and the motion of man's breath. This does not mean that his activities are conceived in precisely the same way by the writer of the Book of Judges, for example, as they are by St. Paul. But all writers believed in a living God who did not merely exist in some remote heavenly abode or manifest himself in certain awe-inspiring cataclysms of the natural order, but who came very near to men, checking them, encouraging them, purifying them, enriching them. In earlier times these activities were conceived in a more direct and impersonal way, in later times in a more complex and personal way, but it was the same God and the same Spirit of God to whom men bore witness. The Spirit who moved upon the waters at creation was the same Spirit who descended upon Jesus in the waters of baptism: the Spirit who empowered Gideon and Saul to become deliverers of their people was the same Spirit who empowered Peter and Paul to be heralds of redemption through Christ. The Divine activity comes gradually to be seen more clearly and understood more fully, but all the biblical writers are concerned to bear witness to the one living God who works in the midst of human life by his Spirit.

THE SPIRIT OF CHRIST

There is one revelation of immense importance in the biblical witness about the Spirit. In the Old Testament we read of this man or that man receiving an access of physical energy or moral power through the Spirit, but there is also a suggestion that something was still lacking. Never had a man appeared in whom the *fullness* of the Spirit had been seen. Where was the man who was both strong to save and wise to rule, instructed in the ways of God and sympathetic to the needs of men, faithful in declaring God's judgement while quick to proclaim God's mercy? Moreover there is a sense that whereas particular individuals may have been conscious of God's power in their lives, the experience had never been a general one. To only a few had the power of the Spirit become a living reality. Hence in the promises of a better time to come, which are so frequently found in the Old Testament, two particular blessings receive special emphasis. One is the hope of the coming of a new leader through whom the Spirit of God could operate without let or hindrance. The other is the hope of a day when the whole community of God's people would be inspired and animated by the living power of God active in their midst. A Spirit-filled leader, a Spirit-inspired community—but when would these hopes be fulfilled?

There can be no shadow of doubt that the profound conviction of the New Testament writers is that the first of these promises had found its fulfilment in the person of Jesus the Messiah, the second in the establishment of the Christian Church. Anointed by the Spirit at his

Baptism, sustained by the Spirit through his Temptation, empowered by the Spirit for his works of healing and his words of salvation, inspired by the Spirit to offer himself willingly to suffering and death, raised in the Spirit to newness of life—in him the life of the Spirit has so been manifested that henceforth it becomes impossible to think of the Spirit apart from Jesus Christ. The Spirit of God *is* the Spirit of Christ. Whatever partial revelations may have been given before, now in one all-embracing revelation the nature of God's activity in the Spirit has been fully disclosed. Nothing incongruous with or incompatible with the Spirit that dwells in Jesus dares lay claim to be a manifestation of the Spirit of God.

Furthermore the New Testament proclaims that the completed work of Christ on earth made possible a more general and more comprehensive bestowal of the Spirit than had ever been known before.

This Jesus—being by the right hand of God exalted, and having received of the Father the promise of the Holy Spirit, hath shed forth this which ye now see and hear.

The Spirit's life and power are available for *all* who turn to Jesus Christ and find in him their Saviour and their Lord. Here is the new commonwealth of those who acknowledge Jesus as Lord through the Spirit (1 Corinthians 12:3), who know God as Father through the Spirit (Galatians 4:6), who discover the true nature of brotherhood through the Spirit (1 Corinthians 12:13). The grace of our Lord Jesus Christ and the love of God and the fellowship of the Holy Spirit is for *all* (2 Corinthians 13:14). This, in short, is the new revelation of the New Testament—that the Spirit of God is only truly known through Jesus Christ, and conversely that *all* who turn to Jesus Christ in faith receive the Spirit of the living God through him.

THE SPIRIT IN ACTION

There are four aspects of the Spirit's activity which receive special emphasis in the New Testament.

1. *The Holy Spirit is the Lord and Giver of Life*. One of man's earliest discoveries must have been that of the close connection which exists between breath and life. To lose breath is to lose life: to breathe steadily and rhythmically is a mark of good health. Man's very life then depends upon the gift of God's breath; and what is true of physical vitality is also true of moral health. When the nation of Israel seemed to be so far away from its true destiny that it could be likened to a collection of dry bones in an open valley, only the coming of the breath of God from the four winds of heaven could restore the people to moral vigour and social integrity.

But in the perspective of the New Testament the life which the Spirit produces is 'life in Christ Jesus' (Romans 8:2). It is a life of moral progress, for he has broken free from the disintegration and decay which are characteristic of sin and death. It is a life of unlimited possibilities of expansion, for 'Christ being raised from the dead dieth no more: death hath no more dominion over him'. He who is related to Christ in the Spirit no longer measures the strength and success of his life by earthly standards but rather by the extent to which he is open to those influences which are ever flowing in from the Spirit who is the Lord and giver of life.

2. *The Holy Spirit is the Source and Generator of Power*. Again man has recognized from very early times that any lack of breath or failure of breath shows itself

immediately in a diminution of strength and energy. He constantly needs power, whether it be to perform the ordinary tasks of life or to face an extraordinary crisis; and it is the consistent testimony of the Bible that this power has been made available to men through the Spirit. It is above all the power of the Spirit that enables men to bear witness boldly to the life and death and resurrection of Christ Jesus in face of ridicule and opposition and persecution and even death. 'Ye shall receive power, when the Holy Spirit comes upon you, and ye shall be my witnesses in Jerusalem and in all Judaea and in Samaria and unto the uttermost part of the earth' (Acts 1:8).

Thus it is the Spirit who strengthens man to resist temptation and to struggle with evil in all its forms. It was in the power of the Spirit that Jesus went to face the temptations of the wilderness. It was in the power of the Spirit that he attacked the forces of evil and cast out demons. It was in the power of the Spirit that he proclaimed the Word of God's deliverance and salvation. There is a group of words associated with the Spirit in the New Testament—different words which may be translated 'strength', 'power', 'energy', 'dynamic force', 'vigour'—all of which testify to the sense of confidence and assurance which animated the early Christians in their struggle with the hostile forces which surrounded them. Without hesitation they attributed this new strength to the power of the Spirit working within them. 'Strengthened with all might according to his glorious power'—this was the condition of men in whom the Holy Spirit was actively present.

3. *The Holy Spirit is the Creator and the Bond of True Fellowship.* It is a striking characteristic of the air we

breathe that it is *common* air. We cannot make a corner in fresh air for ourselves alone. Any group of people, however divergent in other ways, breathe the same air when they gather together in one place. And it can truly be said that one breath animates all the bodies which belong to any one society. In other words it is perfectly natural to conceive of any social group as an organism indwelt by and animated by a single *esprit de corps*.

This image, we find, is taken by St. Paul and applied in the most vivid and detailed way to the social life of the Christian community. It is, he says, like a single Body which has many members, all of which belong to one another within a common pattern of life. In fact the Christian community can aptly be described as the Body of Christ in which all the members share in the one life-giving breath of the Spirit and are united to one another within a fellowship so sensitive that when one member suffers all the members suffer with it, when one member is honoured, all the members rejoice with it. Such a fellowship is a new phenomenon in the world and the quality of its life is represented by a new term which we translate 'love', but which transcends most that is called love in the world today. Love in the New Testament sense is the very life-breath of the fellowship of the Body of Christ. It was he who breathed upon the first group of his disciples and bade them receive this sacred Spirit of love: it was his own Spirit that he gave, and it is only by this Spirit of outpoured love that the Body can live and develop. But when it is thus rooted and grounded in love through the Spirit's glorious energy (Ephesians 3:17) it expands and grows within the bracing atmosphere of the knowledge-surpassing love of Christ and becomes filled with all the fullness of God (Ephesians 3:19).

4. *The Holy Spirit is the Interpreter of Truth and the Guide to the true meaning of Life.* We may be in good health, we may be in full control of our powers, we may be enjoying a harmonious community-life and still we may feel that something is lacking. What does it *mean*? What is the *purpose* of it all? Is there a way to discover the inner secret of this richly-varied universe in which we live and move and have our being? Life without *meaning* can hardly be called life: progress without *purpose* can hardly be called progress.

It is the claim of the Bible that wisdom and insight and understanding are the gift of God to men and that they are mediated by his Spirit. It is not that God gives ready-made answers to all life's questions, but rather that within the developing experience of a personal relationship in the Spirit, God's secrets are gradually unfolded to expectant human hearts. Yet in his mercy God has provided a supreme clue to the meaning of life or, to use another image, a master-key to unlock the doors of life's mysteries: it is the Word who was made flesh and dwelt for a period in our midst. In the pattern of his career, his words, his deeds, his signs, his prayers, his passion, his Cross, his resurrection, we see the true meaning of human life. Through death to life is the final secret of the natural order: through judgement to salvation is the clue to the understanding of the historical order: through sacrifice to wider blessing is the truth of the personal order. All this is the Truth as it is in Jesus, and the New Testament assures us that it is the supreme task of the Holy Spirit to take of the things of Christ and to reveal them to us (John 16:14).

This will be no sudden disclosure. In fact it is clear that the process is still going on. In the noble words which John Robinson spoke to the Pilgrims 'The Lord hath more truth and light yet to break forth out of His Holy Word'. Through successive generations in the history of the Church the Spirit has been glorifying Christ, bringing his words to remembrance, applying them to new situations, guiding men's thoughts and ideas into all truth. Thus the Holy Spirit is the Spirit of Truth, and it is through patient dependence upon him alone that men may enter more deeply into the purpose and meaning of life.

How far now are we justified in speaking of the personality of the Spirit, or of the Person of the Spirit, or of the Spirit as personal? These are exceedingly difficult questions to answer. When we speak of God the Father as personal we think of his relations with Israel and with the prophets and above all with Jesus: these relations must certainly be described as personal, and it does not seem unnatural to speak of the Person of God the Father. When we refer to God the Son as personal we think of his relations with his disciples and with seeking souls and above all with his Father: it does not seem unnatural to speak of the Person of God the Son. But with the Spirit it is different. In ordinary language 'spirit' is not a term which carries the necessary personal reference in the way that 'father' and 'son' do. Moreover, when in ordinary experiences we consider the relation between two persons we do not in any way regard the spiritual bond which binds them together or the perpetual medium through which they communicate with one another as a person. It might perhaps be possible to speak of a child as the personal link between a father and a mother, but then the child has by its very nature a personal existence such as we do not readily associate with 'spirit'. Yet in orthodox Christian theology we are taught that in the unity of the Godhead 'there are three persons of one substance, power and eternity; the Father, the Son and the Holy Ghost'.[1] How are we to understand this?

It does not seem possible to come to a deeper understanding until we recognize that words change their meanings in the course of centuries, and that 'person' as we use it today may not mean exactly the same as the word *persona* did in Latin or as *hypostasis* (the word which the Latin word persona was used to translate) did in Greek. When the early Fathers affirmed that there were three *hypostases* in the Godhead they were emphasizing the fact that the revelation of God as Father, Son and Holy Spirit did not take place through successive manifestations in time, i.e. God did not first show himself as Father, then as Son, then as Holy Spirit. Nor would they have us think merely that God sometimes acts in a fatherly way, sometimes in a filial way and sometimes in an inward spiritual way. Rather the theologians of the Church have been convinced that providential fatherhood belongs to the eternal nature of God as also do sympathetic sonship and sanctifying spirithood. And because God is God and not man, relations are possible between these different characters within God's being which would not be possible between different aspects of a single human personality.

The matter receives some light perhaps when we realize that the oldest use of 'person' in our own language is associated with the 'dramatis personae', the title

[1] Quoted from the 'Athanasian Creed': compare p. 175.

applied to the characters who take part in a play. A 'person' adopts a certain role, represents a certain character, and for the time being he *is* the 'person' of that particular pattern of activity. So even in human experience it is possible for one individual to live and act now as one 'person', now as another. What we acknowledge within the Divine life is that three 'personal' characters belong to the eternal being of God and that ever and always God is acting Father-wise, Son-wise and Spirit-wise. Moreover we confess that within the mystery of the Divine personality there are mutual relations between these three 'persons' of a kind which would be impossible between the various 'persons' which a man might adopt at different periods of his experience. In other words, from all eternity there is personal Fatherhood, personal Sonship and personal Spirithood in God, and mutual personal relationships exist between Father, Son and Holy Spirit within the one communion of love.

The special relevance of all this for our doctrine of the Holy Spirit is that at all costs we must preserve the belief that the Spirit's activities are *personal* through and through. When the Spirit of God enters into human life to sanctify and heal there is no violent coercion, no mechanical manipulation, no magical transformation. The Spirit acts ever to glorify the Father and the Son in their mutual inter-relationship, and his concern is therefore to lead men to the Father through the Son. When the Spirit comes to us he relates us to God himself not by making us conscious of being overborne by an irresistible power or of being lifted up by an irrepressible elation but rather by admitting us to the inestimable privilege of sharing in the mutual love which exists between the Father and the Son within the eternal

M

Godhead. Thus through the Spirit we are being integrated into the very personal life of God himself. The Spirit is personal because the Spirit both acts out the inner personal life of God himself and draws men into participation in that inner personal life. 'The Spirit beareth witness with our spirit that we are the children of God: and if children, then heirs; heirs of God and joint-heirs with Christ; if so be that we suffer with him, that we may be also glorified together.'

PRAYER FOR THE SPIRIT

Whatever difficulties we may have in understanding just what is meant by the 'person' of the Spirit, whatever uncertainties we may have about the ways of his working, nothing need prevent us from joining in the prayer of the Church and of individuals down through the ages —the prayer that the Spirit of God may revive us with life anew, may fill us with fresh power, may pour into our hearts the love of God and of our fellow men, may lead us into all truth. One of the most remarkable of the New Testament pronouncements about prayer is the promise of Luke 11:13. 'If ye then being evil know how to give good gifts unto your children: how much more shall your heavenly Father give the Holy Spirit to them that ask him.'

If then we seek to take this promise seriously, what practical aids may we find in the Book of Common Prayer or a hymnal to assist us in our quest? There is the beautiful supplication at the beginning of the service of Holy Communion that the Spirit may cleanse our hearts; but it is in the services of Confirmation and Ordination that the special prayers for the Spirit's activity are to be found. In the Confirmation prayers we

ask that the candidates may be strengthened with the
manifold gifts of the Spirit, that they may daily increase
in the Holy Spirit and that the Holy Spirit may ever be
with them. At Ordination time the ancient hymn 'Come
Holy Ghost, our souls inspire' is used as a prayer, and
this or its alternative may well be used at any time by
those who desire to experience more fully the presence
and power of 'the fount of life, and fire of love'.
Further, the Collects for Whitsuntide may often be used
in private devotion, as may the terse but richly comprehensive Collect for the Nineteenth Sunday after Trinity:

O God, forasmuch as without thee we are not able to please
thee: Mercifully grant that thy Holy Spirit may in all things direct
and rule our hearts; through Jesus Christ our Lord.

Our hymnals also offer a rich treasury of devotion.
Most of the hymns for Whitsuntide are really prayers
for the guidance and assistance and inspiration of the
Spirit and can articulate our longing that the Holy Spirit
may more fully indwell our individual and corporate
life. In fact few exercises could give a clearer view of the
nature and activity of the Spirit than a careful reading
of these hymns. The burning energy of the Spirit, his
gentle influence, his sanctifying power, his unceasing
illumination, his life-giving breath, his unspeakable love
—these are the gifts about which the hymn-writers sing,
and as we use their songs to express our own aspirations
we shall assuredly be strengthened with might by God's
Spirit inwardly so that Christ will gradually be formed
in us and we shall be filled with all the fullness of God
(Ephesians 3:14–19).

In the early years of this century one of the great
Bishops of the Anglican Communion, Francis J. Cha-
vasse of Liverpool, led a movement of Christians who

banded themselves to pray with special intensity for a
fuller outpouring of God's Spirit upon themselves and
upon his Church. The Bishop himself was like Barnabas
of old 'a good man and full of the Holy Ghost' (Acts
11:24) and his life was a noble inspiration to many.
What was its secret? His son, the present Bishop of
Rochester, has told us that after his father had been
chosen to undertake the great responsibility of the
Liverpool bishopric he withdrew for a period of special
prayer and meditation before his consecration. There in
the quiet one prayer was constantly on his lips. It was a
little couplet which he had composed:

> Spirit, of truth and holiness,
> I pray, not enter, but possess.

Such a prayer will never remain unanswered when it is
the cry of a heart in real earnest. We may ask questions
about the Spirit, we may study his activity in history, we
may wonder about his place in the life of God. All these
are legitimate subjects of inquiry. But in the last resort
it is in prayer and in active witness that we become aware
of the reality and activity of the Spirit. Weak as we are,
'the Spirit helpeth our infirmities': diffident as we are,
the Spirit enables us to speak 'the word of God with
boldness'.

> And every virtue we possess,
> And every victory won,
> And every thought of holiness
> Are his alone.
>
> Spirit of purity and grace,
> Our weakness, pitying see;
> O make our hearts thy dwelling-place
> And worthier thee.

Belief in The Holy Trinity

PERCY HARTILL[1]

WHEN a small child begins to use his powers of reasoning, he concerns himself with some fact and asks 'Why?' And the answer which he expects is one which will link up the fact with something else within his field of knowledge. In other words, he wants to be able to see that fact as an element in a larger unity.

This process, which we see in the child in its simplest form, is in fact the process of all rational thought. The story of Newton and the apple may be true, or it may be legendary: but the supreme importance of Newton's Law of Gravitation was that it enabled us to see that facts as apparently remote from each other as the fall of an apple and the movements of the furthest star are in reality expressions of the same principle. Human thinking is in fact a quest for unity, and our minds can never rest till they have seen all things as elements in a single unity. It may be possible to assert that no such unity exists, but if so all our thinking is invalid, because it rests on an unfounded assumption. Those of us who refuse in this way to dismiss the validity of human thought are obliged to hold that all existence is held together by a single Unity.

Further, our ordinary commonsense tells us that we can only explain anything in terms of what is higher than itself. For example, most of us explain the existence of

[1] See also Archdeacon Hartill's book, *The Unity of God* (Mowbrays).

the plays of Shakespeare by the creative mind of the bard of Stratford: a few people—on what we think inadequate evidence—attribute it to the creative mind of Bacon. But no sane person could suggest that the plays came into being because a chimpanzee arranged the letters of the alphabet in that particular form! In exactly the same way, when we try to explain the existence of the universe, we cannot attribute it to chance or to mere evolution from something lower. We are obliged as rational beings to attribute it to the Creative Mind of One who is at least personal.

Human reason then points to the belief in One Creative Mind, either personal or more than personal—in other words to One God. But the experience shows that few people are guided mainly by reason; and though occasional thinkers here and there were led to a belief in One God (monotheism), the bulk of the human race believed in many gods and goddesses. In pre-Christian history the only striking exception to this was the little race known as the Israelites. They were not a people of philosophers: they did not reach their belief by reasoning: but in their experience they became convinced that there was One God who had made himself known to them, particularly through their leaders and prophets. They used as a sort of creed or watchword of their religion the words 'Hear, O Israel, the LORD our God is one LORD'. By the beginning of the Christian era a number of Gentiles had come to see the reasonableness of this monotheism and had attached themselves loosely to the Jewish community: these were the people known as 'Godfearers', who are more than once mentioned in the Acts of the Apostles. But it was still true that belief in One Creator God was essentially a Jewish conviction.

It was in that Jewish community that Jesus came: and not only did he and his first disciples accept Jewish monotheism without question; he expressly re-affirmed it (St. Mark. 12:29). Belief in One God the Creator is thus the foundation of the Christian Faith, and we must discard at the outset any idea that the doctrine of the Trinity either abandons or modifies it. What we have to ask is 'how did belief in the Trinity arise in this setting of monotheism?'—and what is its significance?

The belief arose because of the emergence of two new facts of which the Jews before the time of our Lord were unaware. The first is the fact of Jesus himself. There is no doubt that in the whole attitude expressed in his recorded teaching he assumed a position in relation to his disciples which was not simply that of a fellow-man. This is not a question of particular texts, in relation to which one can argue endlessly as to whether they are correctly reported or as to what particular words and phrases mean. We are concerned here with what is implicit in the whole of his teaching. Perhaps the best way to realize this is to think of some person whom you intensely admire and who seems to you one of the greatest and best of men, and then to go through our Lord's teaching in any of the Gospels and ask yourself what his words would sound like on the lips of that great and good man. Can we imagine such a person saying 'Come unto me, all that labour and are heavy-laden, and I will give you rest'? Would he have asserted that *everyone* who heard and followed his teaching was like a wise builder, laying sure foundations, and everyone who heard his words and rejected them was like a fool trying to build a house on sand? Would a Francis of Assisi or an Albert Schweitzer have said 'He that loveth father

or mother more than me is not worthy of me'? Would
a Wilberforce or a Shaftesbury have praised those who
gave a cup of water to a needy one *in his name*? Would
a Florence Nightingale have claimed to be the final
judge of her fellows and suggested that the last word of
condemnation was 'Depart from me'? The plain fact is
that the teaching of Jesus as recorded and transmitted
by his followers was of a character that would have
branded anyone else who spoke it as a megalomaniac.
They also believed that he had done wonderful works of
power such as no other could do, and had himself ap-
pealed to those acts as evidence of his Person, though
they rightly held that these acts were not mere 'signs'
in the sense of startling events or super-conjuring tricks,
but were evidence of the quality of his life and work.
And they were certain that after he had been judicially
murdered and the hopes of all his followers had been
shattered, he had risen from the dead and manifested
himself to his friends.

His disciples then were forced to ask themselves 'Who
is this?' They could not believe him to be an impostor,
for the whole quality of his life ruled that out: they
could not regard him as merely a good man, for no good
man could have made such extravagant claims: they
could not think him a megalomaniac (though some of
his contemporaries did) for his simple sincerity made
that explanation impossible. The Fourth Gospel says
that after being convinced of the Master's Resurrection,
the Apostle Thomas cried out 'My Lord and my God!'
The early Christians at first rarely used such explicit
language, but nevertheless they did in fact treat him as
God. And as we observe this fact it is important to remember that these first disciples were not Gentiles who

had previously believed in numerous gods, but Jews nourished in a tradition of One God whose ways are not our ways and whose thoughts are not our thoughts, and who still continued to affirm without qualification that the Lord our God is One Lord. It must have been almost incredibly difficult for convinced Jews to adopt such an attitude to Someone with whom they had been out for walks and sat down to meals; but the strange and important fact is that they *did* adopt this attitude, because the facts compelled them to do so. Jesus was a Person such as they could only treat as God: there was no other way of doing justice to the facts.

One other element in the fact of Jesus must be noted here, because, as we shall see, it is important in the development of the doctrine of the Trinity. The favourite word which he used to describe God was 'Father'. He never used the phrase 'Our Father' so as to include himself and his disciples in the significance of 'our': on the contrary, his language suggests that the relationship between him and his Father was unique. But it does suggest 'relationship'. And this is borne out by the fact that he not only spoke about his father but also spoke *to* him in prayer in the hearing of his friends.

The fact of Jesus then left a problem in the minds of his disciples. On the one hand he had encouraged them to hold fast their traditional Jewish belief in One God, the sole Creator, on Whose will everyone and everything else depend for their very existence. On the other hand they found themselves compelled, in spite of all their natural prejudices, to treat Jesus himself as if he were God, and they felt the need to reconcile this not only with monotheism but with the 'Sonship' of the Father which the Master consistently claimed. Before we consider how Christians dealt with this problem, we must turn to the second new fact which had emerged.

When we examine the life and experience of the early Christian Church as it is described in the Acts of the Apostles and disclosed in apostolic letters, we find that almost equally important with the life, death, and resurrection of Jesus was their conviction that he had bestowed his Holy Spirit on his followers and that they were living under his guidance and direction and were impelled by his power. There is little explicit teaching in these writings as to who this 'Spirit' is, though a great deal is implied. The only place in the New Testament where something like systematic teaching on the subject is given is in the 'last discourse' of our Lord in chapters 14 to 16 of the Fourth Gospel. It lies outside the scope of this essay to discuss how far these chapters represent what Jesus actually said on the day before he was crucified or whether they are the result of a disciple's meditations. But a study of what is implied by the Acts and Epistles in regard to the Holy Spirit leads to the conviction that the Church from the outset held substantially the doctrine which is enshrined in the 'last discourse'; and the only reasonable explanation is that the Church's faith came from the teaching of the Master. We find that the Holy Spirit was not regarded as a force or an influence but always as a Person. It is the masculine pronoun 'he', not the neuter 'it', which is used of him: and this is specially significant in the original Greek, because in that language the word translated 'Spirit' is neuter. He is represented as a Person distinct from the Father and the Son. And a study of the activities attributed to him and the authority which he is recognized as possessing shows that he is regarded as a

Divine Person. Incidental references seem to place him alongside the Father and Jesus Christ with no suggestion of any inferiority or inequality; a notable instance of this is the verse commonly known as 'the Grace' when used in Church services,[1] which forms the conclusion of the Second Epistle to the Corinthians—a letter written at a fairly early date in St. Paul's ministry.

There is one other very important New Testament passage to which we shall return later. So far we observe the Christian Church in its early days springing out of the Jewish faith, firmly holding on to the traditional belief in one God which the Master not only inherited but re-affirmed, and also in practice treating the Master himself as God while recognizing him as other than his Father, and similarly experiencing the Holy Spirit as a Divine Person distinct from them both. At first the Christian community was content to hold on to these convictions without troubling too much to reconcile them with one another or attempting to find a form of words to express their full faith. Sometimes indeed they used language to convey one of these truths which involved a denial of another: for example, one or two early Christian writers spoke of Jesus as a 'second God' —a phrase which, taken literally, involved a repudiation of monotheism; but probably they only meant it to convey that he was God and yet in some sense other than the Father. When, however, the Church spread across the Roman Empire and its new converts came not from the Jewish faith but from heathen religions which worshipped many gods, language of this kind became

---

[1] 'The grace of our Lord Jesus Christ, and the love of God, and the fellowship of the Holy Spirit, be with you all'—from 2 Corinthians 13:14.

dangerous, for ill-instructed converts could easily have regarded Jesus as a kind of second-class god and abandoned entirely the fundamental belief that there is only one God the Creator. So we find a long period of controversy about the Person of our Lord, in which the Church was trying to find a form of words to express that he was God in the proper sense of that word. That is how the phrase emerged which we know in the Nicene Creed—'of one substance with the Father', which simply means 'Just as much God as the Father is', repudiating especially the idea that he was a created being (though of course His *human* nature was created).[1] In these early discussions there was little argument about the Holy Spirit—not that they ceased to believe in him but because they were grappling first with the crucial problem of the Person of Jesus. They were trying to see how (to use the language which became familiar later) there could be two Persons in one God. But later there was a similar controversy about the Holy Spirit, and it was seen that the only way to do justice to the whole of Christian truth was to recognize that God is both Three and One.

At this point we may return to the one New Testament passage which we previously left on one side—the command of the Risen Lord in the concluding verses of St. Matthew's Gospel 'Go ye therefore and make disciples of all the nations, baptising them into the Name of the Father and of the Son and of the Holy Ghost: teaching them to observe all things whatsoever I commanded you: and lo I am with you always, even unto the end of the world; (St. Matthew 28:19–20, Revised

[1] On 'substance' (Greek *ousia*) see also Canon Prideaux's comment, p. 133.

Version). We left this passage aside because some biblical critics have suggested that it does not report an actual
saying of our Lord, but attributes to him what was really
the mind of the early Church. But, as we have seen,
precise trinitarian language is exactly what we do *not*
find in the early Christian writings outside the New
Testament; and nothing is more unlikely than that early
Christian writers should have read back into the mind
of Christ what they themselves had not yet found. The
only reasonable view is that this precise statement came
from our Lord himself, but the Church only gradually
appreciated its significance. The Jews often spoke of the
'Name' of God, meaning his Nature. Here we have the
plain affirmation of the One-ness of God ('Name', not
'Names') alongside the equally plain assertion of his
'three-ness', if one may use the word ('Father, Son and
Holy Ghost'). It thus becomes clear that any statement
which would do justice to the fullness of Christian truth
must find a way of expressing the fact that he is One
and at the same time is Three.

It was only after three or four centuries that the
Church found the language by which this truth could be
expressed and guarded, when it spoke of God as Three
Persons in One Substance. It is often asserted that in
using this language the Church took over the language
and the ideas of Greek philosophy. This is not true: the
particular Greek and Latin words which the Church
used had no clear and distinct meaning in philosophy:
the truth is rather that Christian thinking gave these
words a meaning and significance, which afterwards
contributed much to philosophic thought.

Ordinary Christians however are not concerned about
philosophy. They only want to know what is the meaning

of the rather puzzling language about the Trinity and whether it has any real value for their own contact with God. We have seen already that this language was necessary in order to safeguard different aspects of the truth which Christ revealed: and that is a sufficient justification. But in fact it does two more things. First, it enables us to see something of the richness of the unity of God. We can use the word 'one' with a great variety of meaning. Obviously, we mean more when we speak of the 'unity' of a great work of art than when we speak of the 'unity' of a mathematical point; and we mean still more when we speak of the 'unity' of a great personality. When, therefore, a believer in the Holy Trinity professes belief in the Unity of God, he is not merely asserting the rather negative conviction that there are no other gods; he is also attributing to God the richest possible kind of one-ness.

Secondly, our Christian Faith makes clear precisely wherein this richness lies. When the Latin thinkers of the Church first used the word *persona* or 'Person' of the Father, Son and Holy Spirit, there was no previous use of the word to express what we mean by personality. But already the word was used in its grammatical sense (as we speak of the 'first, or second or third personal pronoun'); and it was a fitting word just because Jesus had revealed what we should call personal relationships within the Godhead. Perhaps the verse in Scripture which sheds the fullest light on the depth of God's Being is the phrase in the High-Priestly Prayer in St. John, chapter 17, where our Lord speaks to his Father of 'the love wherewith thou lovedst me before the foundation of the world'. That shows that God is not merely loving: he is Love. His love is not merely something in his relationship to his creation: it is his own essential nature. It adds much to the spiritual value of our religion that we can sing in the spirit of adoration to the Most Holy Trinity—

'When heaven and earth were yet unmade,
    When time was yet unknown,
Thou, in thy bliss and majesty,
    Didst live and love, alone.'

Now we can understand more clearly the statements of Christian belief concerning the Father, Son and Holy Spirit.

The first of the Thirty-nine Articles, concerning the Holy Trinity, states that, 'There is but one living and true God. . . . And in the unity of this Godhead there be Three Persons, of one substance, power, and eternity: the Father, the Son, and the Holy Ghost'.

And the Athanasian Creed declares that 'we worship one God in Trinity, and Trinity in Unity: neither confounding the Persons, nor dividing the Substance; For there is one Person of the Father, another of the Son, and another of the Holy Ghost; but the Godhead of the Father, of the Son, and of the Holy Ghost is all one, the glory equal, the majesty co-eternal. Such as the Father is, such is the Son, and such is the Holy Ghost. The Father . . . the Son . . . the Holy Ghost, uncreate . . . incomprehensible . . . eternal . . . almighty . . . God . . . Lord, and yet not three Lords, but one Lord. For, like as we are compelled by the Christian verity to acknowledge every Person by himself to be God and Lord, so are we forbidden by the Catholic religion to say there be three Gods, or three Lords. The Father is made of none, neither created nor begotten. The Son is of the Father alone, not made, nor created, but begotten: the Holy

Ghost is of the Father and of the Son, neither made, nor created, nor begotten, but proceeding. So there is one Father, not three Fathers; one Son, not three Sons; one Holy Ghost, not three Holy Ghosts. And in this Trinity none is afore or after other, none is greater or less than another; but the whole three Persons are co-eternal together and co-equal. So that in all things, as is aforesaid, the Unity in Trinity and Trinity in Unity is to be worshipped.'

The Christian Hope

J. E. FISON

HOPE is an important Christian virtue. Much of the hope in the world today, however, is either false or inadequate. There are many, who do not profess Christianity, whose lives are full of hope, and who yet are in no way apparently conscious of their need of Christ and his church. These people are not just escapist 'ivory-tower' theorists. They are in the fore-front of progress. For the physicist, the psychologist and the doctor this is a day of thrilling hope. They may be afraid of the implications of their discoveries, but they cannot but be full of hope, as they advance into the unknown territories, whether of space or of soul, whether of nuclear research or of medical exploration. The astounding advances of science in recent years cannot but inspire a thrilling hope in the minds of many of the best and humblest of our leaders of thought. And it is not only the leaders who have such hope. There is hope in the rank and file as well. The hopes of emigration to a new world on this earth, which inspired England and especially the West Country in the reign of Queen Elizabeth I, are not without their parallel today in the minds of those who plan explorations to other worlds in the reign of Queen Elizabeth II. And in all sorts of other ways hopes are running high—the four-minute mile has been victoriously achieved, the highest mountain of the world has been climbed, and now we face the deepest depth of

N

the sea. We have broken the sound barrier, and now we are up against the heat barrier; we have penetrated into the depths of the sub-conscious mind, and now we hear of the racial unconscious, and begin to wonder where the limits of our personality end. We are tapping energies our fathers never dreamed of, and we are probing mysteries which have been held inviolable since the world began. Space fiction is thrilling our youngsters, and the truth of space-time is stranger than all fiction. In ways like these and in many others, too, hopes are running high outside the Church. And these are hopes, not of the worst, but of the best of our people.

How shall we Christians recapture amid all these worldly hopes the vivid expectation of the early Church? Basically it is by a deeper understanding of, and sharing in, the secret of worship that we shall find the hope we need so badly. Worship is the place where I believe hope will be re-born among Christians today. Ultimately all talk about the future—and all talk about hope must have reference to the future—is valueless and either vain speculation or wishful thinking unless it springs out of the insight and inspiration of worship in the present. It may be a logical scheme, based upon sound intellectual and even biblical argument, but it will have nothing to do with love or with God unless it is born out of that communion with God through Christ here and now, which is the hall-mark both of the genuine Christian prayer meeting and of the genuine Christian eucharist. That was the secret of the hope of the early Church. There was no running away from the present— even to Christ—and there was no clinging on to the past—even to Christ. The first Christians did what they were told to do 'in remembrance of' him, and they found it was not a case of dealing with a distant and receding memory, but with a near and constantly renewed and realized presence. It was out of this realization of Christ's presence that they found the secret of his *parousia*[1] (or final return in glory) which was the nerve of their hope.

If the need of hope among Christians today is indisputable, then the obvious question for us is: How can I find that hope and how can the community of which I am a member find it? Where shall we look for it? The answer is clear and two-fold. We must look for it in the Bible and we must say our prayers to rediscover it for ourselves. We shall not find the secret of the hope we need just by reading the Bible. Constant poring over the texts of the prophets and the evangelists and constant prying into the mysteries of Daniel and Revelation will not by themselves give us that hope—would that some of our most diligent students of prophecy realized this! And, equally, constant attendance at the prayer meeting and even regular participation in the eucharist will not by themselves give us that hope—would that some of our most devout church worshippers realized this! There is no chance of rediscovering the hope of which we are in need, unless we go in for enough serious and up-to-date Bible Study to find out what that hope really is and unless we go in for enough corporate worship and individual prayer to realize it afresh for ourselves. The future we should hope for cannot come alive for us today unless we are worshipping in the eucharist, and it will not live for us today even in the eucharist, unless we are studying the Bible.

[1] *parousia* (Greek) = 'presence' or 'being present' or 'arrival'; this is the word used in the New Testament for the (second) 'coming' of Christ.

First, then, Bible study—what is the object of hope in the Bible? We must begin with the Old Testament, for on this subject ignorance of the Old Testament outlook, in which Jesus himself and all the Apostles were brought up, is largely responsible for cutting the nerve of hope in the Church today. So much is this the case that there seems more real hope among some Jews, who do not know their Messiah, than among many Christians who do.

The Old Testament to begin with offers little hope for individuals after death—and for a very simple reason. It does not think God is concerned with 'the hereafter', and as its hope depends entirely on him, it is not very hopeful about life after death at all. On the other hand from quite early times it does offer hope in this life, at least for the Jews and gradually for others too. The Old Testament is clear that there is a purpose in history and that it is getting somewhere. It is this sense of getting somewhere which filled the Jews with hope. This made them different from all other peoples of the ancient world. Others might be more interested in life after death—the Egyptians certainly were—but they had no sense of history moving anywhere. Everything was like nature and the seasons of the year, going round in circles and getting nowhere. No wonder such an attitude tended to produce a feeling of hopelessness! But the belief that things were getting somewhere—the secret of their hope—was not all plain-sailing for the Jews. The prophets spent a lot of their time roundly denouncing the whole of the popular idea of where they were getting to. They made no bones about it: the popular idea of 'the day of the Lord', the day of Yahweh, was absolute rubbish. But that did not mean there would be no 'day of the Lord', no event towards which everything was moving, no time of final significance approaching and coming nearer with every generation.

On the contrary the prophets agreed with the people that the day of the Lord was coming. It was the day when Yahweh would be up and doing, when he would show his at present largely veiled hand. Of course what you thought about his doings on that day depended on what you thought about his nature today. He would be doing then the things he naturally wanted to do. And about this there were two contradictory ideas; the popular view was that Yahweh wanted to make the Jews 'top nation' and that he would do it on that day. The prophets however had quite different ideas about what he wanted to do and how he would do it. Little by little they realized that his day would not mean a good time for all Jews and a dreadful time for everyone else. It would mean a very bad time indeed for all Jews, who were not good, and it might mean a very good time indeed for Gentiles as well as Jews who were good.

But this hope was not enough, because only the generation alive on that day would ever have its hopes realized. The question had to be faced: What about all those who died before that day? And gradually it began to dawn on the greatest seers of the Jewish people that there was an answer to this question. God was interested in the next life as well as this. Life after death was not going to be just a sort of shadowy going on doing the same things in Sheol as were done on earth. It was meant to be a life of fuller joy and richer experience than could possibly be realized here. So the Jewish hope of life after death was born. If you were in touch with God on earth, death could not break that contact. It was not just a case

of a bit of you going on: it was rather a case of the whole
of you being given a new start in a new life. Eventually,
it was the Jewish belief that the day of the Lord would
mean the resurrection of all the dead and that they would
share with the living in the fulfilment of the purpose of
God which that day would inaugurate. For some it
would be a terrible eye-opener: for others it would be an
indescribably joyful surprise. If we try to discover how
the Jews imagined such a day would happen, first of all
it is clear that they thought it would come about by the
action of God. It was to be the day of his victory, his
V-Day, whatever the means (if any) used to achieve it.
Secondly, while to begin with the idea was that its scope
was limited to the Jews and to those alive on this earth—
and perhaps not all of those—later on it began to be
realized that the day would affect not only all the Jews
but all other people too, not only the whole of the earth,
but the whole universe—and the dead as well as the
living. Thus its significance would be truly cosmic and
its operation would be quite impartial. The notion of 'a
most-favoured-nation treaty' between Yahweh and the
Jews, with a clause in it giving them special privileges
on the day of the Lord, was gradually corrected. The
prophets insisted that special treaties with Yahweh involved special responsibilities rather than special privileges and that, for example, his day would be more
likely to be marked by the fall of Jerusalem than the fall
of Nineveh. No wonder true prophets are never popular,
wherever and whenever they live!

Add one thing more about the day—it was not only
impartial: it was also imminent. The Old Testament
prophets as much as the New Testament apostles are
filled with the notion of an end that is imminent. It is

something that may happen at any moment. There were two reasons for this prophetic insistence on imminence. First of all, as long as there was no belief in a life after death, a hope (or a fear) that was not going to be realized in 'this generation' was irrelevant to 'this generation', except in so far as it unselfishly gave a thought to its successors. Secondly, prophets and seers (like saints) do not work by clock time or think according to calendar time. They know that time is not measured by God in those times at all. It is measured by him in terms of its significance to him. And the imminence of the end is due to the fact that from the Lord's point of view the day of the Lord is overwhelmingly the *most significant* thing that is ever going to happen, even if it is not the *next* thing of any significance at all that is going to happen.

For those who are in love with God—and here we move imperceptibly from the Old Testament to the New —time, as clocks and calendars measure it, is telescoped. It is so real that it flies. It is packed so full of meaning and interest that the end has arrived before you realize it has begun. This is the secret of eternal life, the full meaning of which the New Testament was to reveal, but partial glimpses of which are to be found all through the Old Testament as well. This is what makes the prophets speak of the day of the Lord as always 'just round the corner'. And what about the Messiah in all this? Had he any place on V-Day, and if so, what? To these questions the Old Testament gives different answers in different places. It is quite clear about the day of the Lord, but it is not quite clear how the Lord is going to work on that day. Would he work all on his own by himself, or would he use someone else—some heavenly being, perhaps, or even an earthly man? And if he used

an earthly man, what kind of a man? A king? Yes; but
of what sort? Would he 'throw his weight about' or
would he be 'meek' and 'inherit the earth'? And would
he perhaps mark his day by suffering a defeat rather
than by enjoying a triumph? The Old Testament contains hints like these, but their significance was hardly
ever realized until Jesus came and saw in them the clue
to the real meaning of his life. The expectation of the
day of the Lord was fulfilled and it was fulfilled by the
coming of the Messiah—what we might describe as a prophetic 'aside' was the clue to the fulfilment of prophecy.
And the Messiah who came was a 'meek' Messiah and a
suffering Messiah and a Messiah who 'was crucified,
dead and buried'—this is another prophetic aside, written right away in the margin of the other aside, so much
off the central emphasis of the Old Testament hope that
its significance in chapter 53 of the Book of the Prophet
Isaiah was never seen for hundreds of years till Jesus saw
it and through his own fulfilment of it opened other
people's eyes to it.

So we can sum up the result of the first part of our Bible
study on the hope of the Old Testament. It is not interested in immortality or anything merely individual, as
we ordinarily understand it. But it is interested in resurrection and in judgement and in something truly cosmic.
Its hopes for the future are fixed on the day of the Lord,
which will involve both resurrection and judgement. This
day will have incalculable consequences of weal or woe,
not only for those alive on earth on the day but also for
all who have died before the day. It will affect nature as
well as man, and the entire universe as well as this earth.
It is packed with significance both for the whole universe
and for every individual soul. It is God's V-Day and it is

'just round the corner'. This is the nerve of the Old Testament hope. What does the New Testament make of it?

When we turn from the Old Testament to the New, we are introduced at the outset of the synoptic gospels to a little community on the tip-toe of expectation. 'The kingdom of God is at hand'—that was the message both of John the Baptist and of Jesus himself. And that had been the atmosphere of vivid expectation into which both of them had been born. The Messiah might come at any moment. Was John he? No; but Jesus was. So in fact the great day had arrived: it dawned with 'the voice' of John the Baptist breaking the long centuries of mere echoes of the past. It actually came on the scene— as the sun bursts over the horizon—with Jesus himself. He took up the message of the prophets and proclaimed its fulfilment. He was himself the fulfilment of that message, but to begin with he left his hearers to realize it. He did not shout about himself in so many words: he preached the Kingdom of God and gradually it dawned upon those who heard him that what he was preaching about was something, the meaning of which they could only understand when they looked at him. He was the visible demonstration of the arrival of the Kingdom, whose coming he proclaimed. Of course he completely upset everyone's ideas of what the kingdom meant. Here was God's D-Day, if not his 'V-Day', and it was not going according to their ideas at all. In fact, the whole plan seemed to have completely miscarried when Jesus himself was crucified on the first Good Friday. The disciples, who had never got their Master's meaning clear and had never realized the nature of the victory he was out to win, felt that Good Friday was a complete defeat and the end of all their hopes. But Easter Day proved it was nothing of the kind, and gradually after that it dawned on them that there had been no defeat at all. Everything had gone 'according to plan' and Calvary was at the very heart of the plan. So far so good, and indeed it seemed almost too good to be true— everything that had been hoped for on D-Day and the days after it until V-Day had happened. What was there left in the future for Christians to hope for? Was there, in fact, anything at all left over for them to hope for? The answer to these questions in the New Testament is as clear as it is surprising.

The first Christian community at Jerusalem was quite as much agog with expectation as the little Jewish community into which John the Baptist and Jesus had been born over thirty years before. And this expectation did not die out when the early Church spread through the Gentile world. On the contrary half-way through the first century A.D., within thirty years of the death of Jesus Christ, we find the same vivid expectation in all the Christian communities of the Mediterranean world. The apostles themselves and the Jewish Christians who had known Jesus in Galilee and had forsaken and lost him on Golgotha on Good Friday, and had rediscovered him in the first wonderful forty days after Easter, made no attempt to cling on to their lovely memories of the past. On the contrary, they lived in vivid expectation of the future. And what was true of them was still more true of the Gentile Christians outside Palestine. There was no denying the supreme importance of what had happened in Palestine in the life, death and resurrection of Jesus Christ—the gospels were written in order to insist on that—but there was no trying to cling on to those events in the receding past. The early Christians knew enough of Jesus Christ in worship and prayer in the present not to cling on to the past, but to live for the future. Their knowledge of his presence made them expect his *parousia* (his second coming), and it is the main task of our New Testament study of the nerve of hope to try to understand what that meant.

But first of all we must notice that the whole climate of hope has changed when we move from the Old Testament to the New. In the Old Testament it is the exception rather than the rule to find any clear hope in life after death at all. In the New Testament the old-fashioned Sadducees are the exception to prove the rule that all Jews now believe in life after death. The Gentiles may only have a vague belief in immortality and find Hades a no more inviting prospect than Sheol had been to the Jews. But the Jews are now confidently hoping for the resurrection of the dead. Yet it was not immortality or judgement or even resurrection which was the centre of the Christian hope in the New Testament. That hope still remained fixed on 'the day of the Lord', but there was all the difference in the world between what the day of the Lord meant in the New Testament for the early Christians and what it had meant in the Old Testament for the Jews. The prophets had preached the coming of the day of the Lord. The early Church realized that Jesus was the Lord and soon began to call Sunday 'the day of the Lord', and when they came together to worship on the Lord's day, it was not the day which gripped their minds and fired their imaginations and warmed their hearts; but the Lord. The prophets had spoken of something in the future very different from anything in the present. The early Christians looked for someone in the future whom they already knew in the present. The first Christians were 'in love' with Jesus Christ and that meant that they were 'in Christ'. But to be 'in Christ' did not rule out the vivid hope of one day being 'with Christ, which is far better'. On the contrary, the more they realized his presence every Lord's day, the more they expected his *parousia* on the final Lord's day.

Furthermore, for those who are in love and know the presence, time flies, and so the expectation of the *parousia* is very vivid—it is just as imminent for the early Christians as it had ever been for the Jewish prophets; and it is much more intimate, for the Lord is not now Someone afar off and largely unknown but Someone very near and personally known. He had taught his disciples to pray 'Thy Kingdom come', but the actual words they used were 'Maranatha',[1] 'O Lord, come'. That was the nerve of their future hope. It sprang straight out of their present experience. It was no mere phantasy of the imagination or speculation of the intellect. It was no mere compensation offered in the future to make up for something lacking in the present. Rather, it was the inevitable corollary of the deepest reality of the present. It is the real presence and not the real absence which points to the real *parousia*. What, then, of 'the signs of the times', about which the New Testament says quite a lot, and what of the delay in the *parousia* and what of the almost complete silence of St. John's Gospel about it? If 'the signs of the times' have always so far let

---

[1] *Marana-tha* (see also p. 190), a phrase in Aramaic (the language of Palestine, spoken by Jesus and his first disciples) meaning 'O Lord, come'; it is used by St. Paul, in the original Aramaic, in 1 Corinthians 16:22.

everyone down who had believed in them and have
never yet proved the nearness of Christ's coming, does
not that show the fallacy of the whole *parousia* hope?
Jesus was expected in the first century and he has not
come yet—how can we still believe the *parousia* to be
the nerve of Christian hope? And, anyhow, is there any
need to? Does not St. John re-interpret the whole gospel
so as to show us a 'more excellent way', whereby knowing the presence and the Paraclete[1] we may ignore the
parousia altogether?

This is an easy way out of the difficulty of understanding how it was that the New Testament Christians
hoped for the very thing they had. But to take the easy
way out is to lose the very thing we need. It was because
the New Testament Church knew the presence of love
at the very centre of its life and worship that it looked
for the coming of love and if we have lost the secret of
its hope, the odds are that we have lost the secret of its
love as well. It was because it knew the secret of prevenient grace in the present that it looked for the fulfilment of that secret in the future. It did not invent the
doctrine of the second coming to make up for what was
lacking in the first coming. It expected the *parousia*
because it experienced the presence. And there is no
other legitimate ground for such expectation.

The expectation went back to Jesus himself. Admittedly, as we have seen, he was as silent about the *parousia*
as about the presence and the Paraclete, and it was only
at the very end of his ministry that he let his deepest
secrets out in so many words at all. But the early Church

---

[1] 'Paraclete' is an English form of the Greek word (*paraklētos*) used
in John 14:16 etc. and translated 'Comforter' or 'Advocate' or
'Helper', referring to the Holy Spirit.

grasped those secrets and translated his own words
'Thy kingdom come' into their true meaning, 'Marana-
tha'. They were clear that the real meaning of the arrival
of the kingdom was the coming of the king, and they
went out to convert the world by talking about Jesus
Christ all the time, and by talking about the kingdom
of God hardly at all. If they were troubled by the apparent delay in his coming and invented extra 'signs of the
times' to deal with the problem, it was only because
they did not find it much easier than we do to live in
lovers' time, in which a seven years' engagement can
seem no more than a few days (Genesis 29:20), and in
which eternity is gone in the twinkling of an eye (how
wrong we are about our ideas of 'eternity'!). The
imminence of the *parousia* is reckoned in terms of
lovers' time and for those who are in love its delay is no
problem. But as soon as the early Church fell out of
lovers' time and started reckoning merely by the calendar and the clock, it had to find excuses for the delay in
the fulfilment of its hopes. The nerve of our future hope
is the *parousia* of our Lord, but we shall not discover
that hope for ourselves nor realize its vital nature, if we
merely go in for Bible study. Only as we say our prayers
and share in the worship of the Church, shall we glimpse
out of our experience of the presence something of the
significance of the *parousia*, and begin to see it in its true
perspective and so recapture something of the original
cosmic glory and grandeur of the Christian shape of
things to come.

What then is the form of the future? What is the
Christian shape of things to come? What is the nature
of the Christian hope? Do we see it as an informed hope
or merely as a formless phantom? It is not good enough

for Christians just to share the ancient Greek hope of the immortality of the soul or the modern Marxist hope of the classless society. It is not good enough for Christians just to share the faith of Moslems and Jews in resurrection, judgement, heaven and hell, however improved we may think our version of those doctrines to be. 'There is nothing', as I have written elsewhere, 'distinctively Christian about an outlook on the future, whether of the individual soul or of the world as a whole, which is not centred in Jesus Christ. This is not to deny the importance of immortality, resurrection and the last judgement, but it is to assert emphatically that not one of these doctrines is distinctively Christian at all, however profoundly the Christian gospel may have modified or enhanced its significance. The only distinctively Christian doctrine about the future, which finds expression in the ancient creeds or hymns of the Church, is the terse Latin *Inde venturus*.[1] It is the coming again of Jesus Christ which is at the centre of the Christian hope from the earliest times and it is at its centre, not as the terminus of a movement either of the whole world or of the individual soul towards God, but as the spearhead of God's own loving movement and advance towards the whole world and every single individual soul within it.'[2]

Christians share many doctrines about the past, the present and the future with those who are not Christians, but they view them all in a different light because of their own distinctive convictions. It was the new thing which Jesus Christ brought into the world which altered all the old pattern. And if we ask what that new thing was, we

[1] Quoted from the Apostles' Creed: *Inde venturus est iudicare vivos et mortuos*, 'From thence he shall come to judge the quick and the dead'.
[2] See J. E. Fison, *The Christian Hope* (Longmans).

shall not be far wrong if we say it was the demonstration that God comes to us where we are and as we are, and moves all the way to help us before we take even a step towards him. It is the doctrine of prevenient grace which is the wonder of the incarnation and the atonement and the whole sacramental system of the Church, where that is rightly understood as a visible and effective demonstration and embodiment of the gospel.

This is true now of our present experience. Any desire we have for God, any searching for his truth, any inklings of his love and forgiveness—it is all his doing. He does not shout about what he is up to—love never does —and we can make the great mistake of imagining we are doing it all ourselves. But this is nonsense; it is really all his doing. It is impossible to exaggerate the wonder on a cosmic as well as an individual scale of the divine initiative of love which is at the heart of the Christian good news. This is what we now believe to be true, and if our future hope is related genuinely to our present faith and love, then what God is now up to in the present will give us our clue as to what he will always be up to in the future. He does not change, however much our imperfect and distorted understanding of him needs to change. He was not contradicting at Calvary what he had done at Sinai, and he will not contradict at the end with his *parousia* what he has been doing all the time by his presence. The book of Revelation is no more a literal pre-view of what will happen in the end than is the book of Genesis a literal post-view (if I may use the phrase) of what happened 'in the beginning'. Each gives its own glimpse into either what happened in the beginning or what will happen in the end, and it derives its insight from what is happening now. It is man's present awareness of God and of what he is up to which proves what he was up to 'in the beginning' and what he will be up to in the end. Any doubts about this were settled once and for all by the decisive and final definition of what God is always up to, given by Jesus Christ nearly two thousand years ago. We cannot improve upon that definition, though we are certainly in for some colossal eye-openers as to its full significance. In the light of Jesus's revelation of God, of his gospel of God's coming to men and of his love for sinners and of his initiative and prevenient grace, what form does the shape of things to come assume for the Christian? What is the new thing in the New Testament shape of things to come which distinguishes it from all other outlooks on the future, whether Jewish or Gentile, whether ancient or modern?

The answer to these questions is unmistakable. The only doctrine about the future which enshrines the deepest Christian conviction about the present is the doctrine of the *parousia* of our Lord Jesus Christ. And, significantly, this is the only Christian doctrine about the future which has no parallel in any non-Christian outlook on the future. This is the new thing in the Christian shape of things to come and, if the Christian shape of eschatology (things to come) is not to contradict the Christian shape of the liturgy and the Christian shape of theology itself, this is the key to the nature of hope. Does this, therefore, mean that the Christian 'form' of the future is centred on the sort of fantastic doctrine of the 'second coming', which is preached in some mission halls and seems to dominate some sects? Not at all! The true Christian doctrine speaks of the *parousia* rather than the coming, and the choice of word is significant,

o

for the Greek *parousia* can be translated into English either as 'coming' or as 'presence'. We look for one to come who is present. We are not looking for one to come who is absent. Only those who know his presence will look for his *parousia*. But no one who has any inkling of his presence of love can look for anything else. For it is the *parousia* which alone unifies our outlook on the future. Without it we concentrate either upon what will happen to the individual soul at the end of life after its passage across the stream of time, or upon what will happen to the cosmic process (or some part of it) at the end of history after its passage down the stream of time. Without the *parousia* we either look for the immortality of the soul (and, perhaps, the resurrection of the body) and leave history to take care of itself, or else we look for the end of history (and imagine some blessedness awaiting men at the end) and let every other generation go hang for the sake of the last. The first way is the way of the idealist: the second is the way of the communist. Neither is the way of the Christian.

The Christian is committed to hoping for a future shape of things to come in which both every single individual soul and also the whole cosmic historical process finds its fulfilment. And so long as he looks at that shape from his own standpoint, limited by space and time, such a comprehensive fulfilment is inconceivable. Either the soul or the whole is bound to be disregarded. It is only when he looks at the future in imagination from God's standpoint, which is not limited by space and time, and thinks not of man's approach to God, but of God's approach to man, that he can glimpse the secret of prevenient grace fulfilled and not contradicted at the very end. God comes to meet the individual soul when it passes at death out of time, as we know it, and he comes to meet the cosmic process when it passes at the end of history out of time as we know it. For him it is all one coming, one movement and one meeting. This is no mere meeting of God with the individual soul. The Divine rendezvous is more than a *tête-à-tête*: it is a meeting of God in Christ with all souls and the whole cosmic process of creation as well. It is, perhaps, the final divine return at the end of the divine withdrawal, which opens up the measureless prospects of the 'new heaven' and the 'new earth'. Here is no scrapping of this universe in favour of another, but the transformation of this universe into another. And this, of course, involves the doctrine of the resurrection. But this doctrine is only discussed at length by St. Paul in 1 Corinthians because the Corinthian Church was troubled about the fate of those who died before the *parousia*. He went to great lengths to explain that there was no need to worry: the dead would be raised up and so they would not miss the *parousia* but have as much of a share in it as the living. St. Paul is not nearly so much concerned about the dead going to be with God in another world as about their coming with Christ to this world. This is a startling re-orientation of ordinary thinking, but it is the re-orientation demanded by the New Testament gospel. It is gloriously true that the Christian hope of the resurrection of the body is rooted in the Christian faith in the resurrection of Jesus Christ, to whose body as members of the Church we belong, and therefore Christians have here a future certainty uniquely based upon present fact. But for the Christian, hope in the resurrection should be incidental to hope in the *parousia*.

That meeting is the centre of the Christian hope and the climax not so much of the grand movement of this universe to God as of the gracious movement of God to this universe. God's return to man even more than man's return to God is the final secret of the Christian gospel of love. The heart of our faith is the heart of our hope as well. Of course, this meeting will involve judgement and the judgement will be a great surprise, though for those who know the Judge nothing like the surprise it will be for everyone else. There is no room for either any medieval vindictiveness or any modern sentimentality in his judgement. Nevertheless the purpose of the *parousia* is not just 'to judge the quick and the dead'. The clue to the future is to be found in the present and the clue to the present is to be found in Jesus Christ, and 'God sent not the Son into the world to judge the world; but that the world should be saved through him'. (John 3:17.) What he did, he is doing; and what he is doing, he will do. The present does not reverse the past, and the future will not reverse or contradict the present. Therefore while judgement as well as resurrection have places in the Christian shape of things to come, neither is at the centre and each is seen out of focus unless it is looked at in the light of the *parousia*, which is at the centre.

Finally, we have to consider immortality on the one hand and the millennium and the 'second coming', as the sects understand it, on the other. These doctrines hopelessly distort the Christian shape of things to come, if they are allowed anywhere near the centre of it. But if they know their place—near the outside edge—and keep to it, they have a contribution to make towards the whole picture, which would look the poorer for their absence.

We can now see the importance of the Christian shape of things to come. Everything depends upon the whole being seen in true perspective and right proportion. The *parousia* is at the centre and next to the centre are the resurrection and the judgement and farthest from the centre are immortality on one side and the millennium and the 'second coming' on the other. Seen in right relation to the central *parousia* all other doctrines have some legitimate significance, but they have no specifically Christian significance if seen out of that relation.

The Christian hope is focused on an event and a meeting rather than a state or a vision—and in this it is true to the whole biblical understanding of who God is and of how he reveals himself. Beyond that event and meeting open up the limitless possibilities of both heaven and hell, with all their infinite significance, not only for immortal souls and resurrected bodies but for the whole created universe as well. If this is the nature of the Christian hope, then its secret will only be discovered in prayer and worship. And it will only be discovered in prayer and worship, if these are not escapes from the realities of life, but themselves the deepest realities of life. If through prayer and worship we catch a glimpse of the true significance of life here and now, then that present glimpse of faith and love will open our eyes to the true nature of our future hope. It is the presence of God in Christ realized in prayer and worship which points to his *parousia*. Those who do not know the secret of the presence cannot pry into the secret of the *parousia*, and those who do will not want to.

> Keep Thou my feet; I do not ask to see
> The distant scene; one step enough for me.

CONCLUSION

★

The Place of Understanding

Nathaniel Micklem

THE foregoing chapters have raised more questions than can be summarized or composed in a final essay. I must be content to pick out a few points that seem to me of crucial importance.

First, it must not be claimed by Christians that their doctrines can be proved, nor even that God's existence can be proved. There is no proof that there exists an external physical world round about us except that we are aware of it, and there is no proof of a spiritual or non-physical world round about us except that we are aware of it. By a spiritual or non-physical world about us I mean this, that we are constantly aware of the call of duty, of the appeal of beauty, of the demands of loyalty and the like; these are spiritual awarenesses. In these experiences, as I suppose, we are aware of God. An insect in the sunshine is aware of the sun, though, not being an astronomer, it presumably does not realize that it is of the sun that it is aware. I should claim that all men are aware of God, though many do not realize that it is of God that they are aware.

Religion, as the Dean of St. Paul's says, is *response*; it is response to the spiritual or non-material environment about us or, to put the matter in more usual terms, it is response to God who speaks to us through goodness and beauty and the demands of loyalty and the daily experiences of life. It is the response of our whole nature and not merely of the thinking part of us. It is important to bear this in mind, for the preceding chapters are mostly concerned with the question how we should *think* about our environment.

Second, there is often supposed to be an inevitable quarrel or contradiction between science and religion. The main reason for this is that when a scientist describes and accounts for a rainbow or an eclipse, or when an historian describes and accounts for the Norman Conquest or the French Revolution, he does not bring in the name or thought of God. At the other extreme is the Bible which says, for instance, that God sent a drought to punish the Israelites or God for their sins sent them into captivity, with hardly any references to what we should call natural or historical causes. But is there really a contradiction here?

Let us take as an illustration the blush upon the cheek of Phyllida when Corydon paid her that charming compliment. What caused the blush? A blush is a reddening of the face of which medical men will give you a sufficient and accurate account in terms of the heart and the blood and the corpuscles and so forth. Their account will be true and, as far as it goes, complete. The historian will say that the blush was caused because Corydon made that remark and Phyllida was pleased. True, too, and, so far as it goes, sufficient. The remark, of course, is a physical thing, waves of sound proceeding from the mouth of Corydon and tickling the ear of Phyllida. But a compliment is not waves of sound, it is a notion, an idea, a mental or, if you like, a spiritual thing; the blush, therefore, may truly be described as the result of a non-material or spiritual event acting through the laws of the physical universe. Thus we can give at least three accounts of the blush, a medical, an historical, a mental or 'spiritual', all equally and simultaneously true.

This is a trivial illustration, but it serves to suggest that all events at all times may have a scientific and an historical and a spiritual or non-material explanation, and that when Sir Winston Churchill spoke of our escape from Dunkirk as 'a miracle', he was certainly not contradicting the accounts which scientists and historians must give of it. We are apt to think of miracles as inexplicable breaches of the laws of nature; I suggest, rather, that the laws of nature are never broken, and that God always acts through the laws of his appointment. Archbishop Söderblom of Sweden once said that a miracle is not an event which we do not understand; it is, rather, an event that we do understand, for we never understand fully any event till we see the hand of God in it.

We must see the hand of God in all events or none. To make this point Professor Coulson uses the boldest language; speaking of the sight of a bit of bone-tissue being kept alive in a test-tube he says, 'we don't see what God is like, we actually see God'. He means, if I understand him aright, that we actually see God at work. He does not mean that the bone-tissue is part of God; God, he says later, is 'in the stone, the tree and the clod; but he is also in the very soul of man'.

Third, we must understand the language of religion. If I pour water into a bottle I can say the water is in, that is, is inside, the bottle. But certainly Professor Coulson does not mean that God is inside the stone or tree or clod. So, when the poet says, 'my heart is in the Highlands', we do not understand him to mean that an important part of his anatomy has become mysteriously detached and is operating farther north. We have to use language built up to describe the material, physical world if we are to speak of the spiritual, non-physical world because we have no other language. All religious language must be metaphorical or analogical or mythological. When we speak of God as our Father, we do not mean that we have two fathers in the same sense; when we speak of Christ ascending to heaven, we do not suppose that heaven is a place you can reach if you go far enough up into the sky from the land of Palestine. It is easy to make cheap fun of Christianity if you take its teaching in that literalistic way. A scientific definition which is dealing with this physical world can be exactly, literally and completely accurate. Religious statements cannot be like that. You must try to understand them as you try to understand the poets. Much of the supposed quarrel between science and religion is due to the fact that some scientists (and some theologians) have supposed that religious statements are true in a scientific sense. They may be true in a deeper sense.

Fourth, in the introduction and first two parts of this book questions of astrophysics and creation constantly recur. It is well to be reminded by Professor Hooke that there is in the Bible no one doctrine or theory of creation. 'Creation' is a word that seems necessary though we cannot understand it or explain it. Some modern scientists have been speaking of a constant creation of hydrogen. They must be taken to mean that where there was not hydrogen nor anything to account for hydrogen there mysteriously is hydrogen appearing. The term covers a mystery; it is not an explanation. So when the term 'creation' is used in a religious sense, we do not mean or should not mean, that a Person called God at a certain moment in time produced out of nothing the original atoms or molecules or gases or stardust or what you will, gave the thing a push and started Evolution off upon its way. We are asserting only the mystery that the universe has its origin in the will of God, is held in being by the will of God, and finds its meaning in the will of God. If that be not true, then there is no meaning in anything at all, and reason must give up in despair.

Fifth, if we know anything of God, we know it by revelation. But we need not contrast human discovery with God's revelation. A mathematician, such as Einstein, will wrestle long with a problem, and suddenly the answer, as we say, will dawn upon him. It seems as proper to speak of revelation as of discovery. Revelation means properly an unveiling of that which before was hidden. All discovery is in some sense revelation. In the field of religion we are apt to speak of 'truths of revelation', but it is well that we be reminded by Professor Cairns that in religion revelation does not take the form of propositions as if certain doctrines were mysteriously declared from heaven. It is God who reveals, and it is God who is revealed. The doctrines of religion are the agreed or more or less agreed and necessarily imperfect statements of what is thought to be involved in God's revelation of himself. The self-revelation of God which is distinctive of the Christian religion is in Jesus Christ, not in doctrines about him; the doctrines are but attempts to work out the implications of what the revelation of God in Christ implies.

Sixth, both nature and history represent necessity and

contingency together. The necessary is that which is bound to happen by the laws of nature; the contingent is that which might happen or might not happen. Thus a baby thrush will grow into a big thrush—if a cat does not get it first; an acorn will grow into an oak—unless for some reason it doesn't; Cleopatra's nose, to use the old illustration, will be bound to alter the course of history—unless it gets broken first, as might have happened. Are we, then, to speak of Chance or of Providence? Chance is the opposite of purpose. If anyone can suppose that the development of this planet of ours with its astonishing adaptations of means to ends, its marvels of instinct in the animal world, its gradual evolution of man with his reason, his mental and spiritual life, is just a matter of chance and represents no plan or purpose or mind at all, it will be difficult to argue with him; for that which is due to chance is not due to reason, and he cannot sensibly give reasons for distrusting reason; but if we say that nature and history point to some purpose, and thus speak of Providence, we must not imply that except in the dimmest way we can understand the plan or trace the Providence. What baffles us at every turn is evil. We see nature 'red in tooth and claw', we hear 'the low sad music of humanity', and ask how these things can be if there be a Providence over all and a purpose of good being worked out. About this great human problem too little has been said hitherto, and little can be said now. There is room for two brief observations only.

In the first place, evil is the absence or deprivation of something that ought to be. To be without wings is not an evil in itself; it is an evil for butterflies that ought to have wings, but not for men. To have one leg shorter than another is an evil for a table but not for a kangaroo.

To be a bad character is to fall short of true manhood, what man ought to be, and so on. Evil has no meaning except as a deprivation of something that ought to be in that particular case. In other words, evil presupposes an order of good apart from which there would be no evil. Thus St. Thomas Aquinas rises to his triumphant argument that, if evil is, then God must be. This conception takes us some way, but of course it in no way indicates why there should be any or so much evil in the world.

This is a question that we cannot answer, but, in the second place, we may observe the Christian view that God, respecting the freedom he gave man that we might be real persons and not puppets, does not prevent the evil that we do but is always bringing good out of our evil. This is no doubt a matter of faith and not of proof, but it is a reasonable faith of which the supreme illustration is the death of Christ on the Cross. This was due to a combination of religious bigotry (the Pharisees), worldly judgements and financial interests (the Herodians and Sadducees), power politics (the Roman governor) and the fickleness of the mob. Not only was it a horrible crime in itself but it seemed the final disproof of the goodness and Providence of God of which Jesus had been the Prophet. But because his faith in God and love for men did not fail, God was able to make the Cross the symbol of man's hope, of God's love and of the ultimate victory of God over the sin and evil of the world. Perhaps we do wrong to regard evil as a problem to be solved; it is for us rather an enemy to be overcome.

Seventh, the third part of this book is inevitably written in a somewhat different key from that of earlier sections, for its purpose is to give an account of the great traditional doctrines of the Christian faith as these are propounded by educated and thoughtful men today. The answers are not directly and pointedly related to the questions raised in earlier chapters; moreover, as Canon Prideaux properly observes in one place, 'all this is difficult to understand'. If you ask whether one must understand and accept all this theology before one can be reckoned a proper Christian, the answer must be No. One can be a very great Christian while remaining a most unorthodox theologian; Dr. Albert Schweitzer will here serve as a sufficient illustration. On the other side it must be set that these more theological and dogmatic chapters are dealing with great issues of perennial importance; that they represent the wisdom of powerful and religious minds as interpreted by wise men of the modern world; that great deference is due to this accumulated wisdom; that if in due course having mastered what is here written you should be disposed to disagree, it should be with great hesitation.

Yet these chapters could not have been written fifty, still less three hundred or sixteen hundred years ago, nor, it is to be hoped, could they be written a hundred or two hundred years from now. They express timeless truths in language that has varied and ought to vary from age to age. In other words, theology develops, or ought to develop; the Gospel remains the same.

What, then, is the Gospel? It is not in the least indefinite, but it cannot be neatly and completely and finally defined like a theorem in geometry or a formula in chemistry. It is not a theory or a complex of doctrines; it is, as the name implies, Good News. This Good News is essentially and at every point connected with the coming, the life, the teaching, the death and what happened after the death of Jesus of Nazareth in the first century of our era. It is a story which, if it be true, has tremendous consequences for life. This is one way of telling the story; it begins with the love of God for man which is not to be understood as a vague emotion or general attitude of goodwill but an effective, redeeming love; that man may believe in it, he must see it as an actual, embodied, manifested love, not as a mere idea. This active redeeming love of God for man he has shown in the teaching and in the life of Jesus of Nazareth. Jesus was kind to people. But how deep did the kindness go? Was it without limits? 'Having loved his own he loved them unto the end'—in spite of all that brutality and callousness and shame and horror could bring upon him. He declared the love of God for men; he incarnated the love that he declared, and when he died, it appeared that all his teaching must appear a mockery, for though he had declared the love and care of God for all his children, he himself had died forsaken by his friends and abandoned by God himself. Good Friday seemed the final proof that this is really a God-forsaken world. Jesus did not reveal the character and the love of God unless, after he had shewn this love to the uttermost in the manner of his death, he was vindicated by God himself. Much about what we call the Resurrection is obscure, but what is certain is that many of his followers were convinced that they had seen him after his death and, more important for us, were overwhelmingly aware that God had vindicated Jesus, raised him to be both Lord and Christ, inaugurated a new era as was evidenced in the new spirit of power and love that had come upon them.

It does not sound a very probable story, and it

certainly is not a story that could be proved; but its roots are in quite authentic history. Jesus was a person who taught like that, lived like that, died like that, and after his death the most astonishing things happened— and go on happening. If God's love is an endless and redeeming love, this is how alone it could be shewn; but that does not prove the Resurrection. Was Jesus in the last resort the great deceiver of mankind or the final manifestation of the love of God for man?

That or something like it is the story. It raises for those who accept it all kinds of questions with which theology attempts to deal—how are we to conceive the Person of Christ, how is our forgiveness and reconciliation with God to be understood, how are we to think of the being of God. We must try to understand the implications of the Good News; our theories rest upon it; it does not rest on them.

Our religion is our response to our spiritual or more than natural environment, our response to what God is saying to us through beauty and the demands of loyalty and duty, through the daily experiences of life, through all the prophets and the poets and the scientists and supremely through Jesus Christ. More cannot be required of us than that we be sincere in facing every fact and every challenge life presents to us. Above all, we must be sincere with the fact of Jesus Christ, for either he is the great deceiver or is, as Christians believe, the Way, the Truth, the Life.[1]

This book is primarily concerned with the problems of the mind, but religion is the response of our whole

---

[1] With this question as with almost all the issues raised in this chapter I have dealt somewhat less inadequately in my book *Ultimate Questions* (Geoffrey Bles, 1955).

being. It ought perhaps to be a fact of great religious significance to us that, as I was reading the other day, the average annual income in America is 1,525 dollars and in India is 74, that about half the human race is regularly on the borderline of starvation and is undernourished, that the conditions under which many live in our own land are deplorable, and that we in Britain have responsibilities before God and man for large parts of the world, and that we are far indeed from taking our responsibilities as we ought. No doubt we ought to be more pious than we are; we ought also to be more political and more concerned about our neighbours. True ritual and undefiled is not a matter of theology (though it needs a good theology); it is that a man 'visit the widows and orphans in their affliction and keep himself un-spotted by the world'.[1]

[1] See also by Dr. Nathaniel Micklem: *Religion* (Home University Library, Oxford University Press); *Ultimate Questions* (Geoffrey Bles); and *The Abyss of Truth* (Geoffrey Bles).—Ed.